Microsoft

MOS 2016 Study Guide for Microsoft PowerPoint

Joan E. Lambert

Microsoft Office Specialist
Exam 77-729

MOS 2016 Study Guide for Microsoft PowerPoint

Published with the authorization of Microsoft Corporation by:
Pearson Education, Inc.

ISBN-13: 978-0-7356-9940-3
ISBN-10: 0-7356-9940-2

Library of Congress Control Number: 2016953078

For information about buying this title in bulk quantities, or for special sales opportunities (which may include electronic versions; custom cover designs; and content particular to your business, training goals, marketing focus, or branding interests), please contact our corporate sales department at corpsales@pearsoned.com or (800) 382-3419.

For government sales inquiries, please contact governmentsales@pearsoned.com.

For questions about sales outside the U.S., please contact intlcs@pearson.com.

Editor-in-Chief
Greg Wiegand

Senior Acquisitions Editor
Laura Norman

Senior Production Editor
Tracey Croom

Editorial Production
Online Training Solutions, Inc. (OTSI)

Series Project Editor
Kathy Krause (OTSI)

Compositor/Indexer
Susie Carr (OTSI)

Copy Editor/Proofreader
Jaime Odell (OTSI)

Editorial Assistant
Cindy J. Teeters

Interior Designer/Compositor
Joan Lambert (OTSI)

Cover Designer
Twist Creative • Seattle

Contents

What do you think of this book? We want to hear from you!

Microsoft is interested in hearing your feedback so we can improve our books and learning resources for you. To participate in a brief survey, please visit:

http://aka.ms/tellpress

NC 11.01.2018 1345

3   Insert tables, charts, SmartArt, and media   81

4   Apply transitions and animations   113

What do you think of this book? We want to hear from you!

Microsoft is interested in hearing your feedback so we can improve our books and learning resources for you. To participate in a brief survey, please visit:

https://aka.ms/tellpress

Microsoft Office Specialist

Exam 77-729

PowerPoint 2016: Core Presentation Design and Delivery Skills

This book covers the skills you need to have for certification as a Microsoft Office Specialist in PowerPoint 2016. Specifically, you need to be able to complete tasks that demonstrate the following skill sets:

1. Create and manage presentations
2. Insert and format text, shapes, and images
3. Insert tables, charts, SmartArt, and media
4. Apply transitions and animations
5. Manage multiple presentations

With these skills, you can create and manage the types of presentations that are most commonly used in a business environment.

Introduction

The Microsoft Office Specialist (MOS) certification program has been designed to validate your knowledge of and ability to use programs in the Microsoft Office 2016 suite of programs. This book has been designed to guide you in studying the types of tasks you are likely to be required to demonstrate in Exam 77-729, "PowerPoint 2016: Core Presentation Design and Delivery Skills."

Who this book is for

MOS 2016 Study Guide for Microsoft PowerPoint is designed for experienced computer users seeking Microsoft Office Specialist certification in PowerPoint 2016.

MOS exams for individual programs are practical rather than theoretical. You must demonstrate that you can complete certain tasks or projects rather than simply answer questions about program features. The successful MOS certification candidate will have at least six months of experience using all aspects of the application on a regular basis; for example, using PowerPoint at work or school to create and manage presentations and slides, insert and format slide content (including shapes, text, tables, charts, SmartArt graphics, images, and media), animate slide content, transition between slides, manage multiple versions of a presentation, and prepare presentations for delivery.

As a certification candidate, you probably have a lot of experience with the program you want to become certified in. Many of the procedures described in this book will be familiar to you; others might not be. Read through each study section and ensure that you are familiar with the procedures, concepts, and tools discussed. In some cases, images depict the tools you will use to perform procedures related to the skill set. Study the images and ensure that you are familiar with the options available for each tool.

How this book is organized

The exam coverage is divided into chapters representing broad skill sets that correlate to the functional groups covered by the exam. Each chapter is divided into sections addressing groups of related skills that correlate to the exam objectives. Each section includes review information, generic procedures, and practice tasks you can complete on your own while studying. You can use the provided practice files to work through the practice tasks, and the result files to check your work. You can practice the generic procedures in this book by using the practice files supplied or by using your own files.

Download the practice files

Before you can complete the practice tasks in this book, you need to copy the book's practice files and results files to your computer. Download the compressed (zipped) folder from the following page, and extract the files from it to a folder (such as your Documents folder) on your computer:

https://aka.ms/MOSPowerPoint2016/downloads

> **IMPORTANT** The PowerPoint 2016 program is not available from this website. You should purchase and install that program before using this book.

You will save the completed versions of practice files that you modify while working through the practice tasks in this book. If you later want to repeat the practice tasks, you can download the original practice files again.

The following table lists the practice files provided for this book.

Folder and objective group	Practice files	Result files
MOSPowerPoint2016\Objective1 Create and manage presentations	PowerPoint_1-1.docx PowerPoint_1-2.pptx PowerPoint_1-3a.pptx PowerPoint_1-3b.png PowerPoint_1-4.pptx PowerPoint_1-5.pptx PowerPoint_1-6.pptx PowerPoint_1-7.pptx	PowerPoint_1-1a_results.pptx PowerPoint_1-1b_results.pptx PowerPoint_1-2_results.pptx PowerPoint_1-3_results.pptx PowerPoint_1-4_results.pptx PowerPoint_1-5_results.pptx PowerPoint_1-7_results.pptx
MOSPowerPoint2016\Objective2 Insert and format text, shapes, and images	PowerPoint_2-1.pptx PowerPoint_2-2.pptx PowerPoint_2-3a.pptx PowerPoint_2-3b.jpg PowerPoint_2-4.pptx	PowerPoint_2-1_results.pptx PowerPoint_2-2_results.pptx PowerPoint_2-3_results.pptx PowerPoint_2-4_results.pptx
MOSPowerPoint2016\Objective3 Insert tables, charts, SmartArt, and media	PowerPoint_3-1a.pptx PowerPoint_3-1b.xlsx PowerPoint_3-2a.pptx PowerPoint_3-2b.xlsx PowerPoint_3-3.pptx PowerPoint_3-4a.pptx PowerPoint_3-4b.mp3 PowerPoint_3-4c.mp4	PowerPoint_3-1_results.pptx PowerPoint_3-2_results.pptx PowerPoint_3-3_results.pptx PowerPoint_3-4_results.pptx

Folder and objective group	Practice files	Result files
MOSPowerPoint2016\Objective4	PowerPoint_4-1.pptx	PowerPoint_4-1_results.pptx
Apply transitions and animations	PowerPoint_4-2.pptx	PowerPoint_4-2_results.pptx
	PowerPoint_4-3.pptx	PowerPoint_4-3_results.pptx
MOSPowerPoint2016\Objective5	PowerPoint_5-1a.pptx	PowerPoint_5-1a_results.pptx
Manage multiple presentations	PowerPoint_5-1b.pptx	PowerPoint_5-1c_results.pptx
	PowerPoint_5-1c.pptx	PowerPoint_5-1e_results.pptx
	PowerPoint_5-1d.pptx	PowerPoint_5-2_results.pptx
	PowerPoint_5-1e.pptx	
	PowerPoint_5-2.pptx	

Ebook edition

If you're reading the ebook edition of this book, you can do the following:

- Search the full text
- Print
- Copy and paste

You can purchase and download the ebook edition from the Microsoft Press Store at:

https://aka.ms/MOSPowerPoint2016/detail

Errata, updates, & book support

We've made every effort to ensure the accuracy of this book and its companion content. If you discover an error, please submit it to us through the link at:

https://aka.ms/MOSPowerPoint2016/errata

If you need to contact the Microsoft Press Book Support team, please send an email message to:

mspinput@microsoft.com

For help with Microsoft software and hardware, go to:

https://support.microsoft.com

We want to hear from you

At Microsoft Press, your satisfaction is our top priority, and your feedback our most valuable asset. Please tell us what you think of this book by completing the survey at:

https://aka.ms/tellpress

The survey is short, and we read every one of your comments and ideas. Thanks in advance for your input!

Stay in touch

Let's keep the conversation going! We're on Twitter at:

https://twitter.com/MicrosoftPress

Taking a Microsoft Office Specialist exam

Desktop computing proficiency is increasingly important in today's business world. When screening, hiring, and training employees, employers can feel reassured by relying on the objectivity and consistency of technology certification to ensure the competence of their workforce. As an employee or job seeker, you can use technology certification to prove that you already have the skills you need to succeed, saving current and future employers the time and expense of training you.

Microsoft Office Specialist certification

Microsoft Office Specialist certification is designed to assist students and information workers in validating their skills with Office programs. The following certification paths are available:

- A Microsoft Office Specialist (MOS) is an individual who has demonstrated proficiency by passing a certification exam in one or more Office programs, including Microsoft Word, Excel, PowerPoint, Outlook, or Access.

- A Microsoft Office Specialist Expert (MOS Expert) is an individual who has taken his or her knowledge of Office to the next level and has demonstrated by passing two certification exams that he or she has mastered the more advanced features of Word or Excel.

- A Microsoft Office Specialist Master (MOS Master) is an individual who has demonstrated a broader knowledge of Office skills by passing the Word and Word Expert exams, the Excel and Excel Expert exams, and the PowerPoint, Access, or Outlook exam.

Selecting a certification path

When deciding which certifications you would like to pursue, assess the following:

- The program and program version(s) with which you are familiar
- The length of time you have used the program and how frequently you use it
- Whether you have had formal or informal training in the use of that program
- Whether you use most or all of the available program features
- Whether you are considered a go-to resource by business associates, friends, and family members who have difficulty with the program

Candidates for MOS certification are expected to successfully complete a wide range of standard business tasks. Successful candidates generally have six or more months of experience with the specific Office program, including either formal, instructor-led training or self-study using MOS-approved books, guides, or interactive computer-based materials.

Candidates for MOS Expert and MOS Master certification are expected to successfully complete more complex tasks that involve using the advanced functionality of the program. Successful candidates generally have at least six months, and might have several years, of experience with the programs, including formal, instructor-led training or self-study using MOS-approved materials.

Test-taking tips

Every MOS certification exam is developed from a set of exam skill standards (referred to as the *objective domain*) that are derived from studies of how the Office programs are used in the workplace. Because these skill standards dictate the scope of each exam, they provide critical information about how to prepare for certification. This book follows the structure of the published exam objectives.

See Also For more information about the book structure, see "How this book is organized" in the Introduction.

The MOS certification exams are performance based and require you to complete business-related tasks in the program for which you are seeking certification. For example, you might be presented with a document and told to insert and format additional document elements. Your score on the exam reflects how many of the requested tasks you complete within the allotted time.

Here is some helpful information about taking the exam:

- Keep track of the time. Your exam time does not officially begin until after you finish reading the instructions provided at the beginning of the exam. During the exam, the amount of time remaining is shown in the exam instruction window. You can't pause the exam after you start it.

- Pace yourself. At the beginning of the exam, you will receive information about the tasks that are included in the exam. During the exam, the number of completed and remaining tasks is shown in the exam instruction window.

- Read the exam instructions carefully before beginning. Follow all the instructions provided completely and accurately.

- If you have difficulty performing a task, you can restart it without affecting the result of any completed tasks, or you can skip the task and come back to it after you finish the other tasks on the exam.

- Enter requested information as it appears in the instructions, but without duplicating the formatting unless you are specifically instructed to do so. For example, the text and values you are asked to enter might appear in the instructions in bold and underlined text, but you should enter the information without applying these formats.

- Close all dialog boxes before proceeding to the next exam item unless you are specifically instructed not to do so.

- Don't close task panes before proceeding to the next exam item unless you are specifically instructed to do so.

- If you are asked to print a document, worksheet, chart, report, or slide, perform the task, but be aware that nothing will actually be printed.

- Don't worry about extra keystrokes or mouse clicks. Your work is scored based on its result, not on the method you use to achieve that result (unless a specific method is indicated in the instructions).

- If a computer problem occurs during the exam (for example, if the exam does not respond or the mouse no longer functions) or if a power outage occurs, contact a testing center administrator immediately. The administrator will restart the computer and return the exam to the point where the interruption occurred, with your score intact.

Exam Strategy This book includes special tips for effectively studying for the Microsoft Office Specialist exams in Exam Strategy paragraphs such as this one.

Certification benefits

At the conclusion of the exam, you will receive a score report, indicating whether you passed the exam. If your score meets or exceeds the passing standard (the minimum required score), you will be contacted by email by the Microsoft Certification Program team. The email message you receive will include your Microsoft Certification ID and links to online resources, including the Microsoft Certified Professional site. On this site, you can download or order a printed certificate, create a virtual business card, order an ID card, review and share your certification transcript, access the Logo Builder, and access other useful and interesting resources, including special offers from Microsoft and affiliated companies.

Depending on the level of certification you achieve, you will qualify to display one of three logos on your business card and other personal promotional materials. These logos attest to the fact that you are proficient in the applications or cross-application skills necessary to achieve the certification. Using the Logo Builder, you can create a personalized certification logo that includes the MOS logo and the specific programs in which you have achieved certification. If you achieve MOS certification in multiple programs, you can include multiple certifications in one logo.

For more information

To learn more about the Microsoft Office Specialist exams and related courseware, visit:

http://www.certiport.com/mos

Objective group 1

Create and manage presentations

The skills tested in this section of the Microsoft Office Specialist exam for Microsoft PowerPoint 2016 relate to creating and managing presentations and slides, rather than slide content. Specifically, the following objectives are associated with this set of skills:

1.1 Create a presentation
1.2 Insert and format slides
1.3 Modify slides, handouts, and notes
1.4 Order and group slides
1.5 Change presentation options and views
1.6 Configure a presentation for print
1.7 Configure and present a slide show

You can create PowerPoint presentations from scratch or from a template, or by importing a list of slide titles and content from another file. If you frequently create presentations for a specific purpose, you can efficiently maintain consistent layout and formatting of slides, handouts, and notes by using masters.

Traditionally, presentations are presented electronically as slideshows. You can configure a slideshow that you will present, or for someone else to play locally or online. You can also print presentations and their supporting materials.

This chapter guides you in studying ways of creating and displaying presentations; creating and managing slides; printing presentation content, speaker notes and slide handouts; and configuring and presenting slide shows.

> To complete the practice tasks in this chapter, you need the practice files contained in the **MOSPowerPoint2016\Objective1** practice file folder. For more information, see "Download the practice files" in this book's introduction.

Objective 1.1: Create a presentation

Create a new presentation

When creating a PowerPoint presentation, you have several options, including the following:

- Create a blank presentation that consists only of a title slide, add slides and slide content, and then format the presentation.

- Import a list of slide titles from a text document, add slide content and a title slide, and then format the presentation.

- Import slide titles and content from a Microsoft Word file, add a title slide, and then format the presentation.

- Create a preformatted or prepopulated presentation based on a local or online template.

When PowerPoint is running, you can create a blank or prepopulated presentation from the New page of the Backstage view.

Built-in, online, and custom templates are available from the New page

By default, a new presentation includes only a title slide. You can add blank content slides to the presentation, or copy or move slides from another presentation.

To create a blank presentation

➜ Start PowerPoint. On the start screen, press **Esc** or click **Blank Presentation**.

➜ On the **New** page of the Backstage view, click **Blank Presentation**.

➜ From the program window, press **Ctrl+N**.

Create a presentation based on a template

Creating attractive presentations from scratch can be time-consuming. You can save time by basing your presentation on one of the templates that come with PowerPoint. Two types of templates are available when creating a new presentation:

- **Design template** This is a blank presentation with a theme, and sometimes graphics, already applied to it. Some templates supply only a title slide and leave it to you to add the other slides you need; other templates supply an example of each of the available slide layouts.

- **Content template** From the PowerPoint start screen, you can preview and download presentation templates that are available from the Office website. These templates provide not only the design but also suggestions for content that is appropriate for different types of presentations, such as reports or product launches. After downloading the template, you simply customize the content provided in the template to meet your needs.

To create a presentation based on a template

➜ On the start screen or on the **New** page of the Backstage view, do one of the following:

- Click a featured template. If color options are shown in the preview window, click the color scheme you want, and then click **Create**.

- Double-click a featured template to create a presentation with the default color scheme.

- Enter a template type or subject in the search box, and then press **Enter** or click the **Search** button. Click a template thumbnail to preview its contents, and then create a presentation by clicking **Create** in the preview window; or double-click the template thumbnail to create a presentation without first previewing it.

- Click the **Personal** heading, and then double-click a custom or downloaded workbook template.

Import Word document outlines

To create an unformatted presentation that includes slides, you can import a text file or Word document that contains the slide information. PowerPoint creates unformatted Title And Content slides corresponding to the slide titles specified in the source file.

When creating a presentation from text file content, you can create only slide titles, because text files don't support formatting options that would inform PowerPoint of how you want to use the content. When creating a presentation from Word file content, however, you can format the content by applying multiple heading levels.

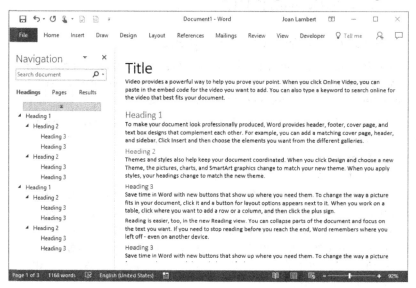

Organize your thoughts in Word and then import the outline to create slides

PowerPoint creates slides, slide titles, and multiple levels of bulleted content based on the heading levels assigned within the Word document. PowerPoint uses only the headings and no other document content. Paragraphs styled as Title or Heading1 become slide titles, and paragraphs styled as Heading2 through Heading9 become bullet points.

If you save an outline containing styled headings as a Word document (.doc or .docx) or a Rich Text Format (RTF) file (.rtf), you can create a new presentation by opening the outline from PowerPoint, or add the outline slides to the existing presentation by importing the outline.

To prepare a Word document as a presentation outline

1. Create a Word document that contains the slide titles and bulleted list content for the slides you want. The document can also contain other content.

2. In the Word document, apply the Title or Heading1 style to text that equates to new slide titles, the Heading2 style to text that equates to first-level bullet points on the slide, and the Heading3 style to text that equates to second-level bullet points. Then save the file.

A slide deck created by importing an outline

To create a presentation based on a Word outline

1. Identify a document that contains the correctly styled outline content.
2. In PowerPoint, do the following:
   a. From the **Open** page of the Backstage view, browse to the folder that contains the Word document.
   b. In the **Open** dialog box, in the **File Type** list, click **All Files** or **All Outlines**.
   c. Double-click the Word document to create a presentation populated with slides corresponding to the slide titles in the document.

To insert slides based on a Word outline into an existing presentation

1. Identify a document that contains the correctly styled outline content.
2. Open the presentation you want to insert slides into.
3. In the **Slides** pane, click to position the insertion bar in the location where you want to insert the new slides.
4. On the **Insert** tab, in the **Slides** group, click the **New Slide** arrow, and then click **Slides from Outline**.
5. In the **Insert Outline** dialog box, browse to the folder that contains the Word document, and then double-click the document to insert slides corresponding to the slide titles in the document.

Objective 1.1 practice tasks

The practice file for these tasks is located in the **MOSPowerPoint2016 \Objective1** practice file folder. The folder also contains result files that you can use to check your work.

➤ Start PowerPoint 2016 and do the following:

❏ Create a new presentation based on the Blank Presentation template. Do not save the presentation.

❏ From within the new presentation, open the **PowerPoint_1-1** document from the practice file folder, to create a presentation based on the outline in the document.

❏ Save the new presentation as <u>PowerPoint_1-1a.pptx</u>.

➤ Start or switch to File Explorer and do the following:

❏ Display the contents of the practice file folder.

❏ Open the **PowerPoint 1-1** document and compare the document to the *PowerPoint_1-1a* presentation to identify the relationship between the outline levels and the slide content.

❏ Close the **PowerPoint 1-1** document and File Explorer.

➤ Open the **PowerPoint_1-1a_results** presentation. Compare the two presentations to check your work. Then close the open presentations.

➤ Return to PowerPoint and do the following:

❏ Create a presentation based on the *Welcome to PowerPoint* template that is available from the New page. If the template isn't in the list, locate it by searching.

❏ Save the new presentation as <u>PowerPoint_1-1b.pptx</u>.

➤ Open the **PowerPoint_1-1b_results** presentation. Compare the two presentations to check your work. Then close the open presentations.

Objective 1.2: Insert and format slides

Add, remove, and hide slides

When you insert a slide into a presentation, PowerPoint inserts it with the default layout immediately after the current slide. If you want to add a slide with a different layout, you select the layout you want from the New Slide gallery. The available layouts and their design depend on the template used to create the presentation.

Thumbnails depict the content of each slide layout

After you insert a slide, you can apply a different layout at any time or, if you make changes to the slide structure, you can reset the layout.

If you want to insert a slide that is similar to an existing slide, you can duplicate the existing slide and then change it instead of having to create the slide from scratch.

If you decide not to include a slide when you deliver a presentation but you don't want to delete the slide entirely, you can hide the slide. Then PowerPoint will skip over that slide during delivery. Hidden slides are still visible in Normal view and Slide Sorter view, but they appear shaded and have a slash through the slide number.

Hidden slide

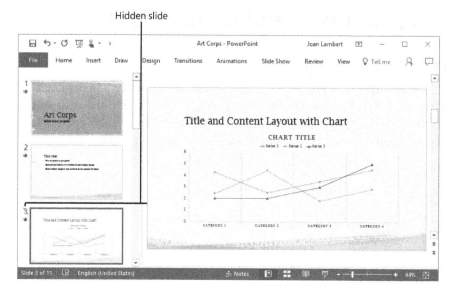

Hidden slides remain in the presentation but aren't shown in a slide show

To add slides

→ In Normal view or Slide Sorter view, click the slide that you want the new slide to follow, and then on the **Home** tab, in the **Slides** group, do one of the following:

- To add a slide of a specific layout, click the **New Slide** arrow, and then click the slide layout you want to add.

- To add a slide of the currently selected layout, click the **New Slide** button or press **Ctrl+M**.

- To add a slide that is identical to the currently selected slide, click the **New Slide** arrow, and then click **Duplicate Selected Slides**.

→ Right-click a slide, and then do one of the following:

- To add a slide of the currently selected layout, click **New Slide**.

- To add a slide that is identical to the currently selected slide, click **Duplicate Slide**.

To apply a slide layout

1. Do either of the following:

   - To apply the layout to only one slide, display the slide in Normal view or select it in Slide Sorter view.

   - To apply the layout to multiple slides, display the presentation in Slide Sorter view, and then select the slides you want to modify.

2. On the **Home** tab, in the **Slides** group, click the **Slide Layout** button, and then click the layout you want to apply.

To reset slide content to the layout defaults

→ Select the slide or slides you want to reset. Then on the **Home** tab, in the **Slides** group, click the **Reset** button.

To hide or unhide slides

→ Right-click a slide or selected slides, and then click **Hide Slide**.

> **Tip** The Hide Slide command name doesn't change; when the selected slide is hidden, the command appears to be selected.

To delete slides

→ Right-click a slide or selected slides, and then click **Delete Slide**.

Format slide backgrounds

You can customize the background of an individual slide by adding a solid color, a color gradient, a texture, or even a picture.

In the Format Background pane, you can specify the colors, texture, pattern, or picture that appear on the background of the current slide or slide master.

You can configure a simple yet elegant slide background by displaying a solid color or color gradient that reflects the color scheme applied to the presentation.

You can configure a more complex slide background by selecting one of the 15 built-in textures or 48 patterns that can be customized with any two colors. Each texture is a small graphic that is tiled on the slide and designed to repeat gracefully, both horizontally and vertically.

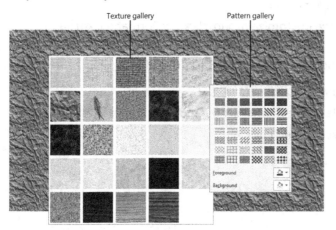

The Paper Bag texture applied to a slide, and other texture and pattern options

If none of the textures meets your requirements, you can tile a picture of your own. You can customize a slide background even further by using a picture as the background. Because most pictures are too busy to support the inclusion of other content on the slide, these are often best used for title slides or other slides that don't have to support a lot of content.

Picture backgrounds can convey additional information on slides with little text

---

Tip If you want to add a watermark, such as the word *Draft* or *Confidential*, to the background of your slides, add the text to the background of the slide master.

To display the Format Background pane

→ On the **Design** tab, in the **Customize** group, click the **Format Background** button.

→ Right-click the slide, and then click **Format Background**.

To modify individual slide backgrounds

1. In Normal view or Slide Sorter view, select the slide or slides you want to modify.

2. Display the **Format Background** pane.

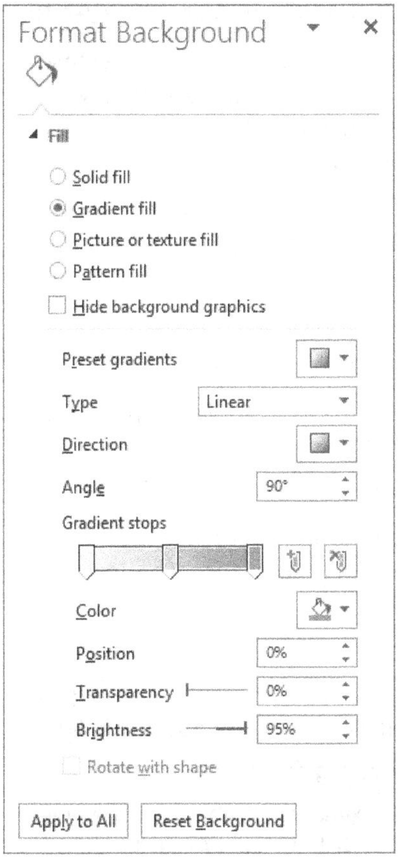

Format Background

▲ Fill

○ Solid fill
◉ Gradient fill
○ Picture or texture fill
○ Pattern fill
☐ Hide background graphics

Preset gradients

Type   Linear

Direction

Angle   90°

Gradient stops

Color

Position   0%

Transparency   0%

Brightness   95%

☐ Rotate with shape

Apply to All   Reset Background

Slide backgrounds can be simple or complex

3. In the **Format Background** pane, do one of the following:

   ● Click **Solid fill**, and then select the color and set the transparency.

   ● Click **Gradient fill**, and then select the type, direction, angle, and gradient stop locations and colors. For each color, set the position, transparency, and brightness.

   ● Click **Picture or texture fill**, and then select a local or online picture, or select a texture. Then set the transparency and if appropriate, select the **Tile picture as texture** check box or set the offset, scale, alignment, or mirror type.

   ● Click **Pattern fill**, and then select a pattern, foreground color, and background color.

4. If you want to remove the background graphics applied by the slide master, select the **Hide background graphics** check box.

5. If you want to apply the background settings to the slide master, click **Apply to All**.

Configure headers and footers on slides and printed materials

To ensure consistency across slides in a presentation, slide header and footer elements are usually managed on slide masters, notes masters, and handout masters. However, you can configure the display of information in slide footers, and in the headers and footers of speaker notes pages and handouts, without modifying the slide master.

The following table describes the information you can display in the slide footer. You have the option of configuring the footer for one slide, for all slides, or for all slides other than the title slide. The footer configuration applies to on-screen and printed slides.

Location	Information
Left side	Static or dynamically updating date and/or time
Center	Text of your choice (approximately 50 characters per line up to 200 characters in the default space)
Right side	Slide number

The following table describes the information you can display on speaker notes pages and handouts. The header and footer configuration applies to the speaker notes pages and handouts for all slides in the presentation.

Area	Location	Information
Header	Left side	Text of your choice (approximately 35 characters per line up to 175 characters in the default space above the slide)
Header	Right side	Static or dynamically updating date and/or time
Footer	Left side	Text of your choice (approximately 35 characters per line extending up from the lower-left corner of the page
Footer	Right side	Page number

To configure slide footer content

1. On the **Insert** tab, in the **Text** group, click the **Header & Footer** button.
2. On the **Slide** tab of the **Header and Footer** dialog box, select the check boxes for the elements you want to display. Options include **Date and time**, **Slide number**, and **Footer**.
3. If you select the **Date and time** check box, do either of the following:
    *   Select the **Update automatically** option, and then select the date and time format you want from the list.
    *   Select the **Fixed** option, and then enter the date and time you want to display.
4. If you select the **Footer** check box, enter the text that you want to display in the center footer section.
5. To suppress the footer elements on the title slide of the presentations, select the **Don't show on title slide** check box.

Selecting an element outlines the corresponding location in the preview area

6. To save your changes, do either of the following:

    - To display the footer only on the current slide, click **Apply**.

    - To display the footer on all slides in the presentation, click **Apply to All**.

To configure notes page and handout header and footer content

1. On the **Insert** tab, in the **Text** group, click the **Header & Footer** button.

2. Click the **Notes and Handouts** tab.

3. Select the check boxes for the elements you want to display. Options include **Date and time**, **Page number**, **Header**, and **Footer**.

4. If you select the **Date and time** check box, do either of the following:

    - Select the **Update automatically** option, and then select the date and time format you want from the list.

    - Select the **Fixed** option, and then enter the date and time you want to display.

5. If you select the **Header** check box, enter the text that you want to display on the left side of the header.

6. If you select the **Footer** check box, enter the text that you want to display on the left side of the footer.

7. To save your changes, click **Apply to All**.

Objective 1.2 practice tasks

The practice file for these tasks is located in the **MOSPowerPoint2016 \Objective1** practice file folder. The folder also contains a result file that you can use to check your work.

➤ Open the **PowerPoint_1-2** presentation and do the following:

❏ Immediately following the title slide (slide 1), insert a new slide with the default *Title and Content* layout. Then, delete the new slide.

❏ After slide 7, insert a new slide with the *Winter Section Header* slide layout. In the title placeholder, enter <u>Winter Wonders</u>.

❏ Duplicate slide 5 (Water Conservation) and then move the duplicate to follow the *Winter Wonders* section opener slide.

❏ Hide the *Falling Rates* section opener (slide 6) and delete the blank slide that follows it (slide 7).

❏ Format the background of only the title slide to display the *Water droplets* texture.

❏ Display slide 3. Change the slide layout from *Picture with Caption* to *Comparison*. Note the effect on the existing slide content.

❏ Configure the slide footer settings to display the footer text <u>My Presentation</u> and the slide number on all slides other than title slides. Then verify that the section openers don't display the footer content.

➤ Save the **PowerPoint_1-2** presentation.

➤ Open the **PowerPoint_1-2_results** presentation. Compare the two presentations to check your work.

➤ Close the open presentations.

Objective 1.3:
Modify slides, handouts, and notes

1

The default content, layout, and formatting of slides within a presentation are controlled at a base level by the slide master. Similarly, the layout and formatting of speaker notes pages are controlled by the notes master, and the layout and formatting of handouts is controlled by the handout master. This topic discusses ways of modifying presentation masters.

Modify slide masters and layouts

When you create a new presentation, its slides assume the formatting of the presentation's *slide master*, which controls the theme and base elements of all the slides. Each slide master is the base for multiple slide templates, called *slide layouts*, which host static content and content placeholders, and control the default formatting of content created within the placeholders.

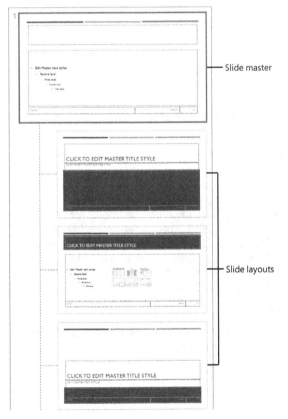

Slide master

Slide layouts

Slide layouts are based on a slide master

Typical slide layouts are Title, Title And Content, Two Content, Section Header, and Blank. Other layouts are specific to the type of content associated with the slide master; for example, the slide master for a photo album might include layouts for Album Cover, Portrait With Caption, or Panorama With Caption.

When working in a presentation, you can change some design elements directly on slides, but changes to the default settings of the presentation can be made only on the slide master and layouts.

You can modify all the slides in a presentation by modifying the slide master on which all layouts are based, or you can modify one type of slide by modifying the layout applied to that slide. If you modify formatting directly on a slide, or insert a slide from another source and want to match it to those in your presentation, you can apply or reset the slide layout to revert its formatting to the default.

You work with slide masters in Slide Master view, which adds a Slide Master tab to the ribbon and hides the tabs that aren't needed. In this view, the slide master thumbnail is displayed at the top of the Overview pane, followed by thumbnails of its associated layouts.

Master elements are managed from the Slide Master tool tab

From the Slide Master tool tab, you can modify elements of the slide master in the following ways:

- Apply a theme or modify the colors, fonts, or effects associated with the current theme.

  Exam Strategy Creating custom color sets, font sets, and themes are part of the objective domains for MOS Exam 77-726, "Word 2016 Expert: Creating Documents for Effective Communication" and MOS Exam 77-728, "Excel 2016 Expert: Interpreting Data for Insights." MOS Exam 77-729, "PowerPoint 2016: Core Presentation Design and Delivery Skill" does not require you to demonstrate the ability to customize theme elements.

- Control the background color, texture, and graphics.

- Specify which placeholders appear on all slides.

- Add custom elements that you want to appear on all slides, including headers, footers, slide numbers, and graphics such as logos.

Changes to the slide master are automatically applied to the connected layouts, and changes to the layouts are applied to the associated slides.

Tip While working in Slide Master view, you can format text placeholders, insert graphic objects, and add animations and transitions by using the same techniques you would use to perform those tasks with slides.

To switch to Slide Master view

➜ On the **View** tab, in the **Master Views** group, click the **Slide Master** button.

IMPORTANT All the following procedures are performed in Slide Master view. You must switch to Slide Master view before you can follow the steps.

To specify the slide layout elements that are controlled by the slide master

1. Select the slide master.
2. On the **Slide Master** tool tab, in the **Master Layout** group, click the **Master Layout** button.

   IMPORTANT The Master Layout button is available only when the slide master is selected. When a slide layout is selected, the Master Layout button is dimmed.

   ---

3. In the **Master Layout** dialog box, select the check boxes of the elements you want the slide master to control. Options include **Title**, **Text**, **Date**, **Slide number**, and **Footer**. Then click **OK**.

These elements can be controlled by the master or delegated to the slide layouts

To change the theme of the slide master and layouts

1. Select the slide master or any associated slide layout.
2. On the **Slide Master** tool tab, in the **Edit Theme** group, click the **Themes** button, and then click the thumbnail of the theme you want to apply to all slide layouts.

To configure the background image on a slide master or slide layout

➜ On the **Slide Master** tool tab, in the **Background** group, click **Background Styles**, and then click the background you want to apply to all slide layouts.

➜ In the **Background** group, click **Background Styles**, and then click **Format Background**. In the **Format Background** pane, configure the fill style, color, and transparency.

➜ To modify the background of the selected slide layout and all other slide layouts, configure the settings in the **Format Background** pane, and then click **Apply to All**.

➜ To remove the slide master background from a selected slide layout, in the **Background** group, select the **Hide Background Graphics** check box.

To insert an image on a slide master or slide layout

1. Do either of the following:
   - Select the slide master to display the image on all associated layouts.
   - Select a slide layout to display the image only on slides with that layout.

2. On the **Insert** tab, in the **Images** group, click **Pictures**.

3. In the **Insert Picture** dialog box, browse to the folder containing the picture you want to insert, click the picture, and then click **Insert**.

4. Move the image to the location you want. Then size and format the picture by using the commands on the **Format** tool tab.

Tip   Use the on-screen guides to align the image with other slide elements.

To add a slide layout to a slide master

➜ On the **Slide Master** tool tab, in the **Edit Master** group, click **Insert Layout**.

➜ Right-click an existing slide layout, and then click **Insert Layout**.

➜ To duplicate an existing slide layout, right-click the slide layout, and then click **Duplicate Layout**.

To display the name and usage of a slide layout

➜ In Slide Master view, point to any slide layout in the **Slides** pane to display the slide layout name and the slides that use the layout.

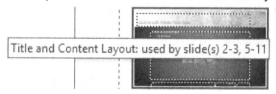

Useful information about a slide layout

To rename a slide layout

1. Right-click the slide layout that you want to rename, and then click **Rename Layout**.

2. In the **Rename Layout** dialog box, replace the current name in the **Layout name** box, and then click **Rename**.

Rename Layout   ?   ✕

Layout name:

Comparison

Rename   Cancel

Slide layout names can reflect their content or purpose

To remove one or more layouts from a slide master

1. In the **Slides** pane, select the slide layout or layouts you want to remove.

2. Do one of the following:

   - Press the **Delete** key.
   - Right-click the selection, and then click **Delete Layout**.
   - On the **Slide Master** tool tab, in the **Edit Master** group, click the **Delete** button.

Tip Only slide layouts that are not currently in use can be deleted. If a slide layout is applied to one or more slides, the Delete Layout command and the Delete button are unavailable.

To insert content placeholders on a slide layout

1. In the **Master Layout** group, click the **Insert Placeholder** arrow, and then click **Content**, **Text**, **Picture**, **Chart**, **Table**, **SmartArt**, **Media**, or **Online Image**.

2. Click the slide to insert a placeholder of the default size and shape, or drag to draw a placeholder of a specific size.

3. Change the size, location, outline, or fill of the placeholder by using the tools on the **Format** tool tab.

To modify placeholders on a slide master or layout

→ Select a placeholder, and then change its size, location, outline, or fill by using the tools on the **Format** tool tab.

→ Select the placeholder content, and then change its font, size, style, effect, and alignment by using commands on the **Home** tab.

To modify a slide layout independent of the slide master

➜ On the **Slide Master** tool tab, in the **Master Layout** group, select or clear the **Title** and **Footers** check boxes to specify whether the slide master sets these elements for the slide master.

➜ In the **Master Layout** group, from the **Insert Placeholder** list, insert the elements for which you want to configure space on the slide layout.

To close Slide Master view

➜ On the **Slide Master** tool tab, in the **Close** group, click **Close Master View**.

➜ On the **View** tab, in the **Presentation Views** or **Master Views** group, click any other view.

➜ On the **View Shortcuts** toolbar at the right end of the status bar, click any view button.

Modify default settings for notes pages

You can print the speaker notes associated with slides as *notes pages*. Notes pages display one slide and the associated notes. There is only one notes master in a presentation.

On the notes master, you can control the page orientation and page background. You can also control whether the following elements appear on the notes pages:

- Slide image
- Speaker notes area
- Header (in the upper-left corner) and footer (in the lower-left corner)
- Date (in the upper-right corner)
- Page number (in the lower-right corner)

You make changes to notes pages from Notes Master view by using the tools on the Notes Master tool tab.

The settings available on the Notes Master tool tab

Tip The theme of the notes pages is set by the presentation. You can change the colors, fonts, and effects that are available to you when formatting the background by selecting them in the Background group.

To switch to Notes Master view

→ On the **View** tab, in the **Master Views** group, click the **Notes Master** button.

To change the page orientation of notes pages

→ On the **Notes Master** tool tab, in the **Page Setup** group, click **Notes Page Orientation**, and then click **Portrait** or **Landscape**.

To specify the elements that appear on notes pages

→ On the **Notes Master** tool tab, in the **Placeholders** group, select or clear the **Header**, **Slide Image**, **Footer**, **Date**, **Body**, or **Page Number** check box.

To format the background of notes pages

→ On the **Notes Master** tool tab, in the **Background** group, click **Background Styles**, and then click the preset background you want to use.

PowerPoint provides 12 background options based on the currently selected color set

Or

1. On the **Notes Master** tool tab, in the **Background** group, click **Background Styles**, and then click **Format Background**.

2. In the **Format Background** pane, configure a solid, gradient, textured, patterned, or picture background just as you would do on a slide.

To change the colors available for background formatting

→ On the **Notes Master** tool tab, in the **Background** group, click **Colors**, and then click the color set you want to use.

To close Notes Master view

→ On the **Notes Master** tool tab, in the **Close** group, click **Close Master View**.

→ On the **View** tab, in the **Presentation Views** or **Master Views** group, click any other view.

→ On the **View Shortcuts** toolbar at the right end of the status bar, click any view button.

Modify default settings for handouts

You can print slides with note-taking space for audience members as *handouts*. Handouts can display one, two, three, four, six, or nine slides. There is one handout master per slide configuration. Changes to any handout master affect all the handout configurations.

On the handouts master, you can control the page orientation and page background. You can also control whether the following elements appear on the handouts:

- Header (in the upper-left corner) and footer (in the lower-left corner)
- Date (in the upper-right corner)
- Page number (in the lower-right corner)

You make changes to handouts from Handout Master view by using the tools on the Handout Master tool tab.

The settings available on the Handout Master tool tab

Tip The theme of the handouts is set by the presentation. You can change the colors, fonts, and effects that are available to you when formatting the handout background by selecting them in the Background group.

To switch to Handout Master view

→ On the **View** tab, in the **Master Views** group, click the **Handout Master** button.

To change the page orientation of all handout configurations

→ On the **Handout Master** tool tab, in the **Page Setup** group, click **Handout Orientation**, and then click **Portrait** or **Landscape**.

To specify the elements that appear on all handout configurations

→ On the **Handout Master** tool tab, in the **Placeholders** group, select or clear the **Header**, **Footer**, **Date**, or **Page Number** check box.

To format the background of all handout configurations

→ On the **Handout Master** tool tab, in the **Background** group, click **Background Styles**, and then click the preset background you want to use.

Or

1. On the **Handout Master** tool tab, in the **Background** group, click **Background Styles**, and then click **Format Background**.

2. In the **Format Background** pane, configure a solid, gradient, textured, patterned, or picture background just as you would do on a slide.

To change the colors available for background formatting

→ On the **Handout Master** tool tab, in the **Background** group, click **Colors**, and then click the color set you want to use.

To preview the effect of changes on different handout configurations

→ On the **Handout Master** tool tab, in the **Page Setup** group, click **Slides Per Page**, and then click **1 Slide**, **2 Slides**, **3 Slides**, **4 Slides**, **6 Slides**, **9 Slides**, or **Slide Outline**.

To close Handout Master view

→ On the **Handout Master** tool tab, in the **Close** group, click the **Close Master View** button.

→ On the **View** tab, in the **Presentation Views** or **Master Views** group, click any other view.

→ On the **View Shortcuts** toolbar at the right end of the status bar, click any view button.

Objective 1.3 practice tasks

The practice files for these tasks are located in the **MOSPowerPoint2016 \Objective1** practice file folder. The folder also contains a result file that you can use to check your work.

➤ Open the **PowerPoint_1-3a** presentation, display Slide Master view, and do the following:

- ❑ Apply the *Slice* theme.
- ❑ On the slide master (not a slide layout), insert the **PowerPoint_1-3b** image from the practice file folder.
- ❑ Position the image so the bottom of the image aligns with the top of the title placeholder and the right side of the image aligns with the right side of the slide number placeholder.
- ❑ Delete the *Name Card Layout*, *Title And Vertical Text Layout*, and *Vertical Title And Text Layout* slide layouts from the slide master.
- ❑ Point to each of the slide layouts to locate the one that is applied to slides 1-4 of the presentation. Duplicate that slide layout.
- ❑ Rename the duplicate as <u>My Slides.</u>
- ❑ On the *My Slides* slide layout, switch the title placeholder and the content placeholder so that the slide title is at the top and the content is centered between the title and footer.
- ❑ On the slide layout that is applied to slides 1-4, hide the background graphics.

➤ Close Slide Master view and do the following:

- ❑ Display slides 1-4 and verify that the background graphic is hidden.
- ❑ Apply the *My Slides* layout to slide 2 and verify that the title and content change places and the background graphic reappears.

➤ Display Notes Master view, and do the following to the notes master.

- ❑ Remove the header and footer placeholders.
- ❑ Apply the *Style 6* background style.
- ❑ Close Notes Master view.

➤ Save the **PowerPoint_1-3a** presentation.

➤ Open the **PowerPoint_1-3_results** presentation. Compare the two presentations to check your work. Then close the open presentations.

Objective 1.4: Order and group slides

To make it easier to organize and format a longer presentation, you can divide it into sections. In both Normal view and Slide Sorter view, sections are designated by titles above the first slide in the section. Section titles do not appear in other views.

Expanded and collapsed presentation sections in Slide Sorter view

You can select, format, move, collapse, expand, and remove sections of slides by selecting the section title and then performing the action. You can print selected sections of a presentation. When collaborating on the creation of a presentation, individual people can edit separate sections.

You can easily reorder the slides within a presentation by moving individual slides or entire sections of slides.

Tip If you arrange open presentation windows side by side, you can drag slides from one presentation to another.

To create presentation sections

1. Do either of the following:

    *   In Normal view, click in the **Slides** pane above the first slide of the new section.

    *   In Slide Sorter view, click in the **Slides** pane to the left of the first slide of the new section.

2. Do either of the following:

    *   On the **Home** tab, in the **Slides** group, click the **Section** button, and then click **Add Section**.

    *   In Normal view, right-click in the **Slides** pane above the slide where you want to begin a new section, and then click **Add Section**.

To rename presentation sections

1. Do either of the following:

    *   Click the section header. On the **Home** tab, in the **Slides** group, click the **Section** button, and then click **Rename Section**.

    *   Right-click the section header, and then click **Rename Section**.

2. In the **Rename Section** dialog box, enter the new section name, and then click **Rename**.

To move slides within a presentation

1. Do either of the following:

    *   In Normal view or Slide Sorter view, select the section headers or thumbnails of the slides you want to move.

    *   In Outline view, select the icons of the slides you want to move.

2. Do either of the following:

    *   Drag the selection to the new location.

    *   Cut the slides from the original location, and then paste them in the new location.

Objective 1.4 practice tasks

The practice file for these tasks is located in the **MOSPowerPoint2016 \Objective1** practice file folder. The folder also contains a result file that you can use to check your work.

➤ Open the **PowerPoint_1-4** presentation and do the following:

- ☐ Divide the presentation into four untitled sections as follows:
  - ○ The title slide and Agenda slide
  - ○ Slides 3 through 6
  - ○ Slides 7 through 10
  - ○ The Summary slide
- ☐ Change the name of the first section to <u>Opening</u>, the second section to <u>Review</u>, the third section to <u>Vision</u>, and the fourth section to <u>Closing</u>.
- ☐ Move the *Vision* section so the sections are in this order: *Opening, Vision, Review, Closing*.

➤ Save the **PowerPoint_1-4** presentation.

➤ Open the **PowerPoint_1-4_results** presentation. Compare the two presentations to check your work.

➤ Close the open presentations.

Objective 1.5:
Change presentation options and views

Display different views of a presentation

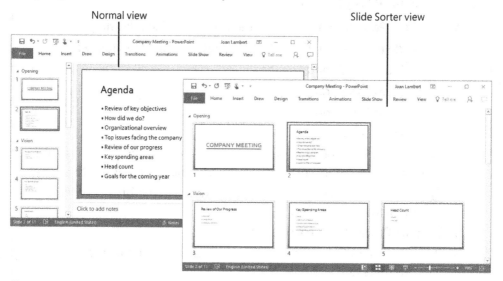

The most common views for working with slide content and presentation structure

PowerPoint has several views in which you can create, organize, and display slides:

- **Normal** This is the default view. You can work with the content of a specific slide and enter development and delivery notes.

- **Slide Sorter** In this view, the slides of the presentation are displayed as thumbnails so that you can easily reorganize them and apply transitions and timings.

- **Reading View** In this view, each slide fills the screen. You use this view to preview the presentation.

- **Slide Show** In this view, each slide fills the screen. You use this view to deliver the presentation to an audience.

- **Notes Page** In this view, each slide is displayed at the top of a page where you can add speaker notes. You can add speaker notes that consist of only text in the Notes pane in Normal view. However, to create speaker notes that contain elements other than text, such as a graphic or a chart, you must be in Notes Page view.

- **Slide Master, Handout Master, or Notes Master** In these views, the masters that control the default design of the presentation components are displayed. You can make changes to the overall design by working with these masters.

See Also For more information about slide masters, handout masters, and notes masters, see "Objective 1.3: Modify slides, handouts, and notes." For more information about notes pages, see "Objective 1.6: Configure a presentation for print." For more information about slide shows, see "Objective 1.7: Configure and present a slide show."

While developing a presentation for which the slides or collateral will be printed, you can display the presentation in monochromatic formats to preview the slide content as it will appear when printed using the Grayscale or Pure Black And White print settings—two of the standard printing options to control the output of color slides on a monochrome printer. This can help to avoid overlapping elements that aren't legible due to similar color tones of the content or the way that the print settings convert the content.

See Also For more information about the Grayscale and Pure Black And White print settings, see "Objective 1.6: Configure a presentation for print."

To display a different view of a presentation

➜ On the **View** tab, in the **Presentation Views** group, click the **Normal**, **Outline View**, **Slide Sorter**, **Notes Page**, or **Reading View** button.

➜ On the **View Shortcuts** toolbar at the right end of the status bar, click the **Normal**, **Slide Sorter**, or **Reading View** button.

To display a presentation as it will print on a monochrome printer

➜ On the **View** tab, in the **Color/Grayscale** group, do either of the following:

- To simulate the Grayscale print setting, click **Grayscale**.
- To simulate the Pure Black And White print setting, click **Black and White**.

Display and edit presentation properties

The properties of a PowerPoint presentation are easily accessible from the Info page of the Backstage view. You can view and modify some properties directly on the Info page, or you can work in the Properties dialog box.

The basic Properties list includes the file size, number of slides, number of hidden slides, presentation title, and tags and categories assigned to the presentation for the purpose of file discovery during a search operation. Statistical file properties (such as number of slides) are generated by PowerPoint and can't be modified. Editable properties include the Title, Tags, and Categories fields. Pointing to the field to the right of an editable property displays an orange box; clicking the box allows you to edit the property.

You can expand the Properties list to display additional presentation statistics and editable properties such as Comments, Status, Subject, Hyperlink Base, and Company.

You can access more properties, including custom properties that might be specific to your organization's file storage requirements, in the file's Properties dialog box.

To access presentation properties

→ The basic **Properties** list is on the **Info** page of the **Backstage** view.

→ To expand the **Properties** list, click the **Show All Properties** link below the list.

→ To open the **Properties** dialog box, do either of the following:

- On the **Info** page of the Backstage view, click **Properties**, and then click **Advanced Properties**. Editable properties are located on the **Summary** and **Custom** tabs of this **Properties** dialog box.

- In File Explorer, right-click the file, and then click **Properties**. Editable properties are located on the Details tab of this Properties dialog box.

To set or change basic properties

1. In the **Properties** list, click an editable property field to activate it.

2. Select existing text that you want to replace. Placeholder prompts such as Add A Tag disappear automatically.

3. Enter the information you want to assign to the property.

4. Press **Enter** or click away from the property field.

Change slide size

By default, PowerPoint 2016 slides are sized for a widescreen display (13.333 inches by 7.5 inches). The slides are oriented horizontally, with slide numbers starting at 1. You can set the size and orientation of the slides, and the orientation of notes, handouts, and outlines, to fit your intended distribution methods. You modify these attributes in the Slide Size dialog box.

The Slide Size dialog box

Exam Strategy Exam 77-729, "PowerPoint 2016: Core Presentation Design and Delivery Skills," requires you to demonstrate the ability to change among standard and custom slide sizes. Changing the orientation of slides and printed collateral is not part of the exam objective domain.

You can select from the following slide sizes:

- **On-screen Show** For an electronic slide show on screens of various aspects (4:3, 16:9, or 16:10)
- **Letter Paper** For a presentation printed on 8.5-by-11-inch US letter-size paper
- **Ledger Paper** For a presentation printed on 11-by-17-inch ledger-size paper
- **A3 Paper, A4 Paper, B4 (ISO) Paper, B5 (ISO) Paper** For a presentation printed on paper of various standard international sizes
- **35mm Slides** For 35mm slides to be used in a carousel with a projector
- **Overhead** For transparencies for an overhead projector
- **Banner** For a webpage banner
- **Widescreen** For a widescreen monitor display
- **Custom** For slides that are a nonstandard size

Tip The Custom setting is particularly useful if you use PowerPoint to create something other than slide presentation. For example, I lay out the art elements for postcards, brochures, and posters on custom-sized PowerPoint slides, and save the slides as PDF files to print.

Each presentation has only one slide size—a presentation can't contain slides of different sizes. Changing the slide size of a presentation can affect the appearance of slide content, particularly when the slide height or width decreases. Accordingly, you have two options for the scaling of existing content: Maximize and Ensure Fit.

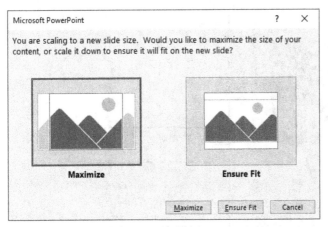

The Ensure Fit option scales all slide content to fit the slide

The scaling options gracefully handle text and image content on the slides, but images, shapes, or other objects located on the slide masters can become skewed. It's important to review slide content after changing the slide size so you can address any content that didn't maintain its aspect ratio (the height-to-width relationship) when it was scaled. You might need to manually rescale images that are part of the slide master.

To change the slide size of a presentation

1. On the **Design** tab, in the **Customize** group, click the **Slide Size** button, and then do either of the following:

    -   On the **Slide Size** menu, click **Standard (4:3)** or **Widescreen (16:9)**.
    -   On the **Slide Size** menu, click **Custom Slide Size**. In the **Slide Size** dialog box, do either of the following, and then click **OK**:
        -   In the **Slides sized for** list, select the size you want.
        -   In the **Slides sized for** list, click **Custom**. Then in the **Width** and **Height** boxes, specify the slide dimensions you want.

2. In the **Microsoft PowerPoint** dialog box that opens, click **Maximize** to ensure that no blank space is added to the slide, or **Ensure Fit** to ensure that all existing content fits on the slide.

To manually rescale an image or object on a slide master

1. Display the presentation in Slide Master view.
2. Display the slide master or associated slide layout that contains the skewed image, and select the image or object.
3. On the **Format** tool tab, click the **Size** dialog box launcher to display the Size & Properties page of the Format *Object* pane.

Incorrect scaling of a square image

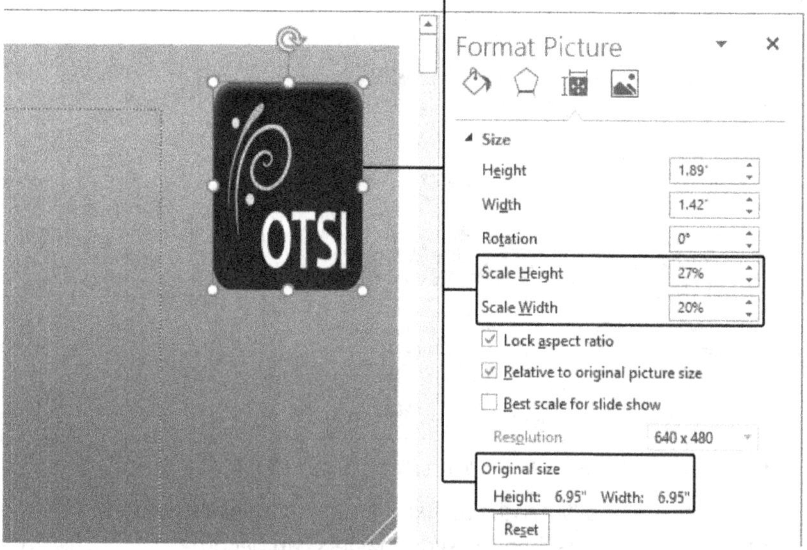

Slide scaling can affect the aspect ratio of slide master images

4. Set the **Scale Height** and **Scale Width** to the same percentage.
5. Close Slide Master view.

Objective 1.5 practice tasks

The practice file for these tasks is located in the **MOSPowerPoint2016 \Objective1** practice file folder. The folder also contains a result file that you can use to check your work.

➤ Open the **PowerPoint_1-5** presentation and do the following:

- ☐ Review the slide content, specifically noting the appearance of the image on slides 3, 4, and 5.
- ☐ Display the Properties list and expand it to show all properties. Change the Title property to <u>Vacation Ideas</u> and set the Status property to <u>In Progress</u>.
- ☐ Display the presentation in Slide Sorter view.
- ☐ Set the slide size for the presentation to *On-screen Show (4:3)*, and choose the option to maximize the slide content. Notice the effect of this selection on the text on slide 2 and the image on slides 3 through 5.
- ☐ Undo the slide size change. Then reselect the slide size, and click the Ensure Fit option.
- ☐ Set the slide size for the presentation to *On-screen Show (4:3)*, and choose the option to ensure the fit of slide content. Notice the effect of this selection on the slide content and the difference between the two fit options.
- ☐ Manually rescale the image on the slide master, setting the Scale Height to match the Scale Width. Ensure that the image is vertically aligned with the content placeholder, and then close Slide Master view.
- ☐ Display the presentation as it would appear in grayscale, and then as it would appear in black and white. Notice the changes required to make the presentation content visible and effective in each of those color schemes.

➤ Save the **PowerPoint_1-5** presentation.

➤ Open the **PowerPoint_1-5_results** presentation. Compare the two presentations to check your work.

➤ Close the open presentations.

Objective 1.6:
Configure a presentation for print

A PowerPoint presentation can include many types of information; the information on the slides is intended for the audience, and the information stored in the slide notes is usually intended for the presenter.

Tip If you use speaker notes when delivering a presentation to an audience, you can enter text in the Notes pane in Normal view. If you want speaker notes that include pictures or other supporting materials in addition to text, you can develop the speaker notes in Notes Page view.

You can print various forms of the presentation for different purposes. You can select from standard print layout options for slides, notes pages, outlines, and handouts.

Print Layout

Full Page Slides	Notes Pages	Outline

Handouts

1 Slide	2 Slides	3 Slides
4 Slides Horizontal	6 Slides Horizontal	9 Slides Horizontal
4 Slides Vertical	6 Slides Vertical	9 Slides Vertical

✓   Frame Slides
✓   Scale to Fit Paper
   High Quality
   Print Comments and Ink Markup

Options for printing slides, notes, and handouts

When you are ready to print, you can adjust any of the following settings:

- **Specify the printer to use** You can specify the printer you want to use and set its properties (such as paper source and image compression).

- **Specify which slides to print** You can print all the slides, the selected slides, or the current slide. You can print only specific slides by clicking the Slides box and entering slide numbers and ranges separated by commas (no spaces). For example, enter *1,5,10-12* to print slides 1, 5, 10, 11, and 12.

- **Print hidden slides** You can include slides in the printed version that will be hidden in the electronic presentation.

- **Specify what to print** You can print slides (one per page), notes pages (one half-size slide per page with space for notes), an outline, or handouts. When printing handouts, you can specify the number of slides that print on each page (1, 2, 3, 4, 6, or 9) and the order in which the slides appear on the page.

- **Put a frame around slides** You can print a frame around the slides on the printed page.

- **Scale slides to fit the paper** If you haven't set the size of the slides to match the size of the paper in the printer, PowerPoint can automatically reduce or increase the size of the slides to fit the paper when you print them.

- **Print in high quality** For final output, you can specify that the slides be printed in the printer's highest quality.

- **Print comments and ink markup** You can print electronic or handwritten notes attached to the presentation so that you can review them along with the slides.

- **Print and collate multiple copies** If you want to print multiple copies of a presentation, you can specify whether complete copies should be printed one at a time.

- **Specify the color range** You can print your presentation in color (color on a color printer and grayscale on a monochrome printer), grayscale (on a color or monochrome printer), or pure black and white (no gray on either a color or monochrome printer).

Tip Most presentations are created in color. The Grayscale option prints grayscale versions of the colors, but the Pure Black And White option removes colored backgrounds. Be sure to review the presentation in the print mode you select before printing it to ensure that all the necessary content is visible.

To print all or part of a presentation

→ On the **Print** page of the Backstage view, do any of the following, and then click **Print**:

- In the first list in the **Settings** area, click **Print All Slides**, **Print Selection**, or **Print Current Slide**.

- In the first list in the **Settings** area, click **Custom Range** and then, in the **Slides** box, enter the slides you want to print.

- In the **Slides** box, enter the slides you want to print.

The Print page of the Backstage view

To print speaker notes

→ On the **Print** page of the Backstage view, in the second list in the **Settings** area, in the **Print Layout** gallery, click **Notes Pages**. Configure any additional print settings, and then click **Print**.

To print handouts

→ In the second list in the **Settings** area, in the **Handouts** gallery, click the hand-out configuration you want. Configure any additional print settings, and then click **Print**.

To configure print colors for a presentation

→ On the **Print** page of the Backstage view, in the final list in the **Settings** area, click **Color**, **Grayscale**, or **Pure Black and White**.

Objective 1.6 practice tasks

The practice file for these tasks is located in the **MOSPowerPoint2016 \Objective1** practice file folder.

➤ Open the **PowerPoint_1-6** presentation and do the following:

❑ Review the presentation content, noting the slides that contain speaker notes.

❑ Print full page slides of only slides 1-3, using the Color setting.

❑ Print a full set of handouts (for all slides) with three slides per page, using the Grayscale setting.

❑ Print a set of speaker's notes, double-sided if your printer supports it, using the Pure Black And White setting.

➤ Close the **PowerPoint_1-6** presentation without saving changes.

Tip There is no result file for this set of practice tasks because the tasks don't modify the presentation content.

Objective 1.7:
Configure and present a slide show

You can deliver a presentation as an on-screen slide show, starting either from the beginning or from the current slide. If you're presenting from your computer on a remote monitor, you can display the slides to the audience but see upcoming slides and your slide notes on your computer by using Presenter View. You can use Presenter view to display the current slide, slide notes, next slide, and slide controls in one window, whether on the same monitor or on a separate monitor.

Current slide   Current slide notes   Next slide

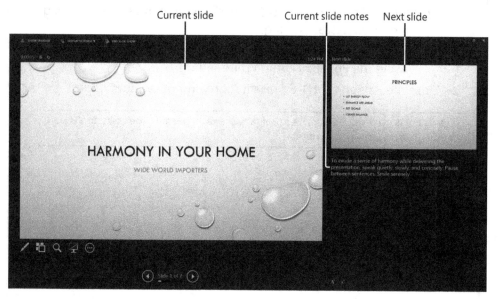

Presenter View is a valuable tool

Tip Presenter View is also useful when you're reviewing or rehearsing timings for a slide show.

When you're preparing to deliver a slide show, you can configure the slide show settings to reflect the environment in which it will be presented. In the Set Up Show dialog box, you can specify the following:

- How the presentation will be delivered
- Whether all slides will be shown, or only a subset of the available slides
- Whether an automatic slide show will loop continuously, be shown without narration, and be shown without animation
- Whether slide timings will be used
- Whether your hardware setup includes multiple monitors and, if so, whether you want to use Presenter view

- What pen color and laser pointer color you want to use

You can control various presentation options for a slide show without having to modify the presentation

When delivering a slide show, you can move from slide to slide in the following ways:

- **Manually** You control when you move by clicking the mouse button, pressing keys, or clicking commands.
- **Automatically** PowerPoint displays each slide for a predefined length of time and then displays the next slide.

For automatic slide shows, the length of time a slide appears on the screen is controlled by the slide timing that you configure. You can apply timings to a single slide, to a group of slides, or to an entire presentation, either by allocating time to each slide or by rehearsing the presentation while PowerPoint automatically tracks and sets the timings for you.

You can rehearse slide timings for your own information or to automate slide movement

While delivering a presentation, you can direct attention to specific content by using the on-screen pointer, or reinforce your message by drawing or highlighting specific text on slides.

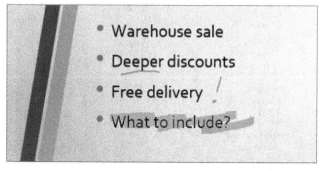

Mark up presentations to keep the audience engaged

The pen color is determined by a setting in the Set Up Show dialog box, but you can easily change the pen color during the presentation.

If you need to deliver variations of a presentation to different audiences, you can maintain one presentation containing all the slides you are likely to need for all the audiences. Then you can select the slides that are appropriate for a specific audience and assign them to a custom slide show.

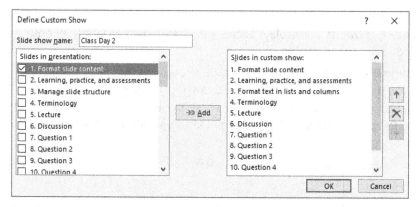

PowerPoint renumbers slides in the custom show so gaps aren't apparent to the audience

To set up a slide show

1. On the **Slide Show** tab, in the **Set Up** group, click the **Set Up Slide Show** button.
2. In the **Set Up Show** dialog box, do any of the following, and then click **OK**:
   - In the **Show type** area, select the method of delivery.
   - In the **Show options** area, select the check boxes of the options you want to use, and select the pen and laser pointer colors from the menus.

- In the **Show slides** area, indicate whether you want to display the entire presentation, selected slides, or a selection that you've already assigned to a custom slide show.
- In the **Advance slides** area, select the method by which you want to move through the slide show.
- In the **Multiple monitors** area, if you're displaying the slide show on a monitor or display device other than the one from which you're delivering it, select that device in the **Slide show monitor** list and select the screen resolution at which you want to display the slide show in the **Resolution** list. If you want to display the presenter notes on one monitor and the slide show on the other, select the **Use Presenter View** check box.

To start a slide show from the first slide

➜ Do either of the following:

- On the **Slide Show** tab, in the **Start Slide Show** group, click **From Beginning**.
- On the **Quick Access Toolbar**, click the **Start From Beginning** button.
- Press **F5**.

To start a slide show from the current slide

➜ Do either of the following:

- On the **Slide Show** tab, in the **Start Slide Show** group, click **From Current Slide**.
- Press **Shift+F5**.

To run a custom slide show

➜ On the **Slide Show** tab, in the **Start Slide Show** group, click the **Custom Slide Show** button, and then click the custom slide show you want to run.

Or

1. In Slide Show view, move the mouse to display the navigation toolbar in the lower-left corner.
2. On the navigation toolbar, click the **Navigation** button (labeled with an ellipsis), click **Custom Show**, and then click the show you want.

To move between slides

➜ To move to the next slide, do any of the following:

- Click the current slide.
- Right-click the slide, and then click **Next**.
- On the navigation bar, click the **Advance to the next animation or slide** button (labeled with a right-pointing arrow).
- Click the **N**, **Enter**, **Page Down**, **Right Arrow**, **Down Arrow**, or **Spacebar** key.

→ To move to the previous slide, do any of the following:

- Right-click the slide, and then click **Previous**.
- On the navigation bar, click the **Return to the previous animation or slide** button (labeled with a left-pointing arrow).
- Click the **P**, **Page Up**, **Left Arrow**, **Up Arrow**, or **Backspace** key.

→ To move to a specific slide, do any of the following:

- Enter the slide number, and then press **Enter**.
- In Presenter view, click the **See all slides** button, and then click the slide.
- To return to the beginning of the presentation, point to the presentation screen, and then press and hold both mouse buttons for two seconds.

To display a slide show in Presenter view on your monitor

1. Start the slide show.
2. On the navigation toolbar in the lower-left corner of the screen, click the **Options** button (labeled with an ellipsis) and then click **Show Presenter View**.

To display Presenter view on one monitor and a standard slideshow on another

1. In the **Set Up Show** dialog box, in the **Multiple monitors** area, in the **Slide show monitor** list, click the monitor on which you want to display the slides to the audience.
2. Select the **Show Presenter View** check box, and then click **OK**.
3. Switch to Slide Show view. Then on the control monitor, use the **Presenter** view tools to control the presentation.

Or

1. On the **Slide Show** tab, in the **Monitors** group, in the **Show Presentation On** list, click the monitor on which you want to display the slides to the audience.
2. In the **Monitors** group, select the **Use Presenter View** check box.
3. Switch to Slide Show view. Then on the control monitor, use the **Presenter** view tools to control the presentation.

To use the on-screen pen, highlighter, or laser pointer

1. Do any of the following:

- In Slide Show view, on the navigation toolbar, click the **Pen** button, and then click **Pen**, **Highlighter**, or **Laser Pointer**.
- To change the pointer to a pen, press **Ctrl+P**.
- To change the pointer to an arrow, press **Ctrl+A**.
- Right-click anywhere on the screen, click **Pointer Options**, and then click **Pen**, **Highlighter**, or **Laser Pointer**.

2. Use the tool to annotate the slide or draw attention to specific content.

3. Turn off the tool by changing the pointer to an arrow.

Tip When the pen, highlighter, or laser pointer tool is active in Slide Show view, clicking the mouse button does not advance the slide show to the next slide. You need to switch back to the regular pointer to use the mouse to advance the slide.

To rehearse slide show timings

1. Display the first slide of the presentation.

2. On the **Slide Show** tab, in the **Set Up** group, click the **Rehearse Timings** button.

3. Rehearse the presentation, advancing the slides at the appropriate times.

4. When the slide show ends, click **Yes** in the **Microsoft PowerPoint** dialog box that opens, to save the recorded slide timings and apply them to the slides.

Tip To restart the timing of a specific slide, on the Recording toolbar, click the Repeat button to reset the time for that slide to 0:00:00. To start the entire rehearsal over again, click the Close button on the Recording toolbar, and then click No in the message box that prompts you to keep the timings.

To create a custom slide show

1. On the **Slide Show** tab, in the **Start Slide Show** group, click the **Custom Slide Show** button, and then click **Custom Shows**.

2. In the **Custom Shows** dialog box, click **New**.

> **Tip** To create a custom slide show that is similar to an existing custom slide show, click the slide show, click Copy, and then edit the copy.

3. In the **Define Custom Show** dialog box, enter a name for the custom show in the **Slide show name** box.

4. In the **Slides in presentation** list, select the check boxes of the slides you want to include in the custom slide show, and then click **Add**.

5. In the **Slides in custom show** list, select any slide you want to reorder, and then click the arrows to reorder the slides.

6. In the **Define Custom Show** dialog box, click **OK**.

7. In the **Custom Shows** dialog box, click **Close** to return to the presentation or click **Show** to run the custom slide show.

Objective 1.7 practice tasks

The practice file for these tasks is located in the **MOSPowerPoint2016 \Objective1** practice file folder. The folder also contains result files that you can use to check your work.

➤ Open the **PowerPoint_1-7** presentation and do the following:

❑ Start the slide show, and then switch to Presenter View and move to slide 3.

❑ Set the pen color to bright blue, and then underline the word *shared* on slide 3.

❑ On slide 3, erase the line under the word *shared*. Then highlight the word in light green.

❑ On slide 6, use a red pen to draw circles around the two instances of *External* and the word *internal*.

❑ End the slide show and retain the annotations. Save the annotated presentation as <u>MyNotes.pptx</u>.

➤ Return to the **PowerPoint_1-7** presentation and do the following:

❑ Rehearse the timings for the presentation, spending as much time on each slide as it takes for you to read the content. Save the slide timings.

❑ Create a custom slide show named <u>Managers</u> that includes slides 1, 3, 4, 5, 7, and 10.

❑ Play the *Managers* slide show.

❑ Edit the *Managers* slide show to add slide 11.

➤ Save the **PowerPoint_1-7** presentation.

➤ Open the **PowerPoint_1-7_results** presentation. Compare the two presentations to check your work.

➤ Close the open presentations.

Objective group 2
Insert and format text, shapes, and images

The skills tested in this section of the Microsoft Office Specialist exam for Microsoft PowerPoint 2016 relate to inserting and formatting text, shapes, and images. Specifically, the following objectives are associated with this set of skills:

2.1 Insert and format text

2.2 Insert and format shapes and text boxes

2.3 Insert and format images

2.4 Order and group objects

The most important part of a PowerPoint presentation is the content. Slide content traditionally consists of bullet points, but there are other ways of presenting text and enhancing slides with imagery to avoid the monotony of endless bulleted lists.

This chapter guides you in studying ways of inserting, formatting, linking to, ordering, and grouping text and images on slides.

To complete the practice tasks in this chapter, you need the practice files contained in the **MOSPowerPoint2016\Objective2** practice file folder. For more information, see "Download the practice files" in this book's introduction.

Objective 2.1: Insert and format text

Insert text on a slide

When you add a new slide to a presentation, the slide layout you choose uses place-holders to indicate the type and position of the objects on the slide. You can enter text directly into a text placeholder on a slide when you're working in Normal view, or you can enter it in the Outline pane when you're working in Outline view.

If you need to insert text outside of the provided placeholders, you can insert a text box on the slide and then enter the text in the text box. The text box content will use the default font set provided by the presentation theme.

See Also For information about inserting text boxes on slides, see "Objective 2.2: Insert and format shapes and text boxes."

Format text on a slide

The default formatting of text in placeholders reflects the design of the underlying slide master. You can use standard character and paragraph formatting techniques to override the following aspects of the design, or to format text that isn't controlled by placeholders:

- **Alignment** You can align the text horizontally to the left, right, or center; or you can justify it to span the text box. You can align the text vertically at the top of the text box, in the middle, or at the bottom.
- **Case** You can make selected text all lowercase or all uppercase; ensure that the text is capitalized as a sentence or that each word has an initial capital letter; or change the capitalization of each letter.
- **Character spacing** You can make the space between characters looser or tighter.
- **Color** Picking a color from the applied color scheme creates a pleasing design impact. You can also add colors that are not part of the color scheme, including colors from the standard palette or from the almost infinite spectrum of colors available in the Colors dialog box.
- **Direction** You can rotate text or stack the letters on top of each other.
- **Fancy text effects** You can apply fancy effects such as shadows, reflections, and bevels, or rotate or mold text into a shape.
- **Font and size** You can pick a different font or size for any selection.
- **Indentation** You can indent the text from the left side of the text box.
- **Line and paragraph spacing** You can adjust the vertical spacing.
- **Style and effects** You can apply simple styles such as bold and italic, or you can choose more dramatic effects such as shadows, colored underlining, or small caps.

Exam Strategy PowerPoint responds differently to the way you enter text depending on where you are entering it. Become familiar with the different ways of creating new text and bulleted list levels so that you can enter text efficiently during the exam.

You format text content by using the commands in the Font and Paragraph groups on the Home tab of the ribbon, many of which are also on the Mini Toolbar that temporarily appears when you select text.

You can access additional settings in the Font and Paragraph dialog boxes. PowerPoint doesn't have as many font or paragraph formatting options as are available in Word, but you can achieve most effects.

PowerPoint has simpler text formatting options

After you format one text selection to suit your needs, you can quickly apply the same combination of formatting to another selection by using the Format Painter. You can also clear all manual formatting from a selection so that it reverts to the formatting specified by the design.

To change the font of selected text

➔ On the **Mini Toolbar** or in the **Font** group on the **Home** tab, click the font you want in the **Font** list.

To change the size of selected text

➔ On the **Mini Toolbar** or in the **Font** group on the **Home** tab, click the **Increase Font Size** or **Decrease Font Size** button.

➔ On the **Mini Toolbar** or in the **Font** group on the **Home** tab, in the **Font Size** list, click a specific point size.

To change the case of selected text

→ On the **Home** tab, in the **Font** group, click the **Change Case** button, and then click the option you want.

→ Press **Shift+F3** to cycle among the case options.

To change the color of selected text

→ On the **Mini Toolbar** or in the **Font** group on the **Home** tab, click the color you want in the **Font Color** palette.

Or

1. Display the **Font Color** palette, and then click **More Colors**.
2. On either the **Standard** or **Custom** tab of the **Colors** dialog box, specify the color you want, and then click **OK**.

To change the font style or effect of selected text

→ On the **Mini Toolbar** or in the **Font** group on the **Home** tab, click the button for the style you want.

Or

1. On the **Home** tab, click the **Font** dialog box launcher.
2. In the **Font** dialog box, specify the style or effect you want, and then click **OK**.

To change the character spacing of selected text

→ On the **Home** tab, in the **Font** group, click the **Character Spacing** button, and then click **Very Tight**, **Tight**, **Normal**, **Loose**, or **Very Loose**.

Or

1. On the **Home** tab, in the **Font** group, click the **Character Spacing** button, and then click **More Spacing**.
2. On the **Character Spacing** tab of the **Font** dialog box, in the **Spacing** list, click **Normal**, **Expanded**, or **Condensed**.
3. Change the **By** setting to the precise amount of space you want between characters, and then click **OK**.

To change the alignment of selected text

→ On the **Mini Toolbar** or in the **Paragraph** group on the **Home** tab, click the **Align Left**, **Center**, **Align Right**, or **Justify** button.

→ Press **Ctrl+L** to left-align text, **Ctrl+E** to center text, **Ctrl+R** to right-align text, or **Ctrl+J** to justify text.

→ On the **Home** tab, in the **Paragraph** group, click the **Align Text** button, and then click the vertical alignment you want.

To change the indentation of selected text

➜ On the **Mini Toolbar** or in the **Paragraph** group on the **Home** tab, click the **Increase List Level** or **Decrease List Level** button.

Or

1. On the **Home** tab, click the **Paragraph** dialog box launcher.
2. In the **Paragraph** dialog box, in the **Indentation** area, change the **Before text** setting, and then click **OK**.

To change the line spacing of selected text

➜ On the **Home** tab, in the **Paragraph** group, click the **Line Spacing** button, and then click the spacing you want.

Tip Clicking Line Spacing Options displays the Paragraph dialog box.

Or

1. On the **Home** tab, click the **Paragraph** dialog box launcher.
2. In the **Paragraph** dialog box, in the **Spacing** area, change the **Before** or **After** settings, or the **Line Spacing** option, and then click **OK**.

To change the direction of text in a placeholder

➜ Click anywhere in the placeholder, and on the **Home** tab, in the **Paragraph** group, click the **Text Direction** button, and then click the direction you want.

To copy existing formatting to other text

1. Select the text that has the formatting you want to copy.
2. On the **Mini Toolbar** or in the **Clipboard** group on the **Home** tab, do either of the following:
   - If you want to apply the copied formatting only once, click the **Format Painter** button once.
   - If you want to apply the copied formatting multiple times, click the **Format Painter** button twice.
3. Click or select the text to which you want to apply the copied formatting.
4. If you clicked the **Format Painter** button twice, click or select each additional text segment you want to format. Then to turn off the Format Painter, click the **Format Painter** button again, or press the **Esc** key.

To clear all manual formatting from selected text

➜ On the **Home** tab, in the **Font** group, click the **Clear All Formatting** button.

➜ Press **Ctrl+Spacebar**.

Create WordArt

WordArt is a term for sets of text effects that you can apply directly to text and independent objects that have those effects applied. These effects can include outlines, fills, shadows, reflections, glow effects, beveled edges, and three-dimensional rotation. You can modify the effects whether they are applied directly to text or to WordArt objects.

Become a Microsoft Office Specialist!

A simple WordArt object

When creating a WordArt object, you start by choosing one of the 20 built-in WordArt styles. When applying WordArt formatting, you can start from one of the built-in styles or build your own combination of text fill, outline, and effects.

Independent WordArt objects exist in their own text boxes and can be positioned and formatted independently of other slide content. You create and format WordArt containers and text by using commands on the Format tool tab.

You format WordArt object containers by using the Shape commands

To create an independent WordArt object

1. On the **Insert** tab, in the **Text** group, click the **WordArt** button, and then click the WordArt style you want.

2. Replace the *Your text here* placeholder text in the WordArt object with the text you want.

Tip You can set the font, size, weight, and other attributes of WordArt text as you would with any other text.

To apply WordArt formatting to existing text

1. Select the text that you want to format.

2. On the **Format** tool tab, in the **WordArt Styles** group, do either of the following:

   - Expand the **Quick Styles** gallery and then click the preconfigured effect combination you want to apply.

   - From the **Text Fill**, **Text Outline**, and **Text Effects** menus, apply your own combination of formatting.

Text fill options   Text outline options   Text effect options

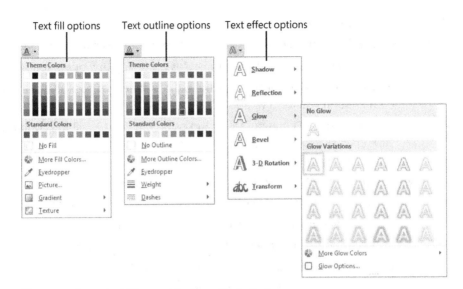

You can easily create striking combinations of text effects

Tip The color scheme of the WordArt styles and style elements is provided by the presentation theme. If you change the theme or color scheme, your WordArt and other presentation elements remain coordinated.

To format WordArt text

1. Select the WordArt object and click the **Format** tool tab if it isn't active.
2. On the **Format** tool tab, in the **WordArt Styles** group, do any of the following:
   - In the **WordArt Quick Styles** gallery, click the built-in style you want to apply.
   - From the **Text Fill** menu, select the color you want to apply to the text.
   - On the **Text Outline** menu, do any of the following:
     - Select the color you want to apply to the text outline.
     - Click **Weight**, and then click the outline weight (thickness) you want.
     - Click **Dashes**, and then click the outline pattern you want.
   - On the **Text Effects** menu, click any of the following, and then click the setting you want to apply to the WordArt text:
     - Shadow
     - Reflection
     - Glow
     - Bevel
     - 3-D Rotation
     - Transform

To format a WordArt object container

1. Select the WordArt object and click the **Format** tool tab if it isn't active.

2. On the **Format** tool tab, in the **Shape Styles** group, do any of the following:

    -   In the **Shape Styles** gallery, click the built-in style that has the outline and fill combination you want to apply.

    -   From the **Shape Fill** menu, select the color you want to fill the container with, or click **Picture**, **Gradient**, or **Texture**, and then select the related option you want to use.

    -   On the **Shape Outline** menu, do any of the following:

        ○   Select the color you want to apply to the container outline.

        ○   Click **Weight**, and then click the outline weight (thickness) you want.

        ○   Click **Dashes**, and then click the outline pattern you want.

    -   On the **Shape Effects** menu, click any of the following, and then click the setting you want to apply to the WordArt text:

        ○   Preset

        ○   Shadow

        ○   Reflection

        ○   Glow

        ○   Soft Edges

        ○   Bevel

        ○   3-D Rotation

To change the shape of the WordArt object container

1. Select the WordArt object and click the **Format** tool tab if it isn't active.

2. On the **Format** tool tab, in the **Insert Shapes** group, click **Edit Shape**, click **Change Shape**, and then click the shape you want the container to be.

Tip You change the location, size, position, text wrapping, and other characteristics of a WordArt object by using the same techniques as with other graphic elements.

Format text as bulleted or numbered lists

Bulleted lists form the foundation of most presentations. You can enter up to nine levels of bullets in a content placeholder. By default, the bulleted list items you enter are all first level, but you can easily demote and promote list item levels, both on the slide and in Outline view.

If you have entered regular text paragraphs in a placeholder or an independent text box, you can convert the text to a bulleted list or a numbered list. You can also convert a bulleted list or numbered list to regular text paragraphs.

The appearance of the bullet characters for each list level is determined by the formatting prescribed on the slide master. However, you can customize a bulleted list by using basic formatting techniques. You can also change the size, color, and symbol of the bullets. For a numbered list, you can change the number scheme and the size and color of the numbers.

2

Classical composers

♪ Renaissance era
♪ Baroque era
　♫ Bach
　♫ Handel
　♫ Vivaldi
♪ Classical era
　♫ Haydn
　♫ Mozart

♪ Romantic era
　♫ Beethoven
　♫ Chopin
　♫ Liszt
　♫ Wagner
♪ Modernist era
　♫ Debussy
　♫ Strauss
　♫ Stravinsky

Custom bullets can accentuate slide content

For both types of lists, you can specify the indenting of each level. If you want to adjust the indenting of multiple levels, it is best to start with the lowest level and work your way up, using equal increments. Otherwise you might end up with a list that looks uneven and unprofessional.

See Also For information about formatting bulleted list items as SmartArt diagrams, see "Objective 3.3: Insert and format SmartArt graphics."

To convert selected text to a bulleted list

➜ On the **Home** tab, in the **Paragraph** group, click the **Bullets** button.

To change the bullets in a selected bulleted list

➜ On the **Home** tab, in the **Paragraph** group, click the **Bullets** arrow, and then click the bullet style you want.

Or

1. On the **Home** tab, in the **Paragraph** group, click the **Bullets** arrow, and then click **Bullets and Numbering**.

2. On the **Bulleted** tab of the **Bullets and Numbering** dialog box, change the size and color of the existing bullet.

Select from hundreds of bullet symbols and specify the size and color

3. To change the bullet symbol, click **Customize**, choose a font and symbol in the **Symbol** dialog box, and then click **OK**.

4. To use a picture as a bullet, click **Picture**, and then in the **Insert Picture** dialog box, locate and double-click the picture file you want.

5. Click **OK** to close the dialog box and apply the change.

To convert selected text to a numbered list

→ On the **Home** tab, in the **Paragraph** group, click the **Numbering** button.

To change the numbers in a selected numbered list

→ On the **Home** tab, in the **Paragraph** group, click the **Numbering** arrow, and then click the standard numbering style you want.

Or

1. On the **Home** tab, in the **Paragraph** group, click the **Numbering** arrow, and then click **Bullets and Numbering**.

2. On the **Numbered** tab of the **Bullets and Numbering** dialog box, change the size and color of the number.

3. If you're continuing a list from another slide, enter or select the starting number in the **Start at** box.

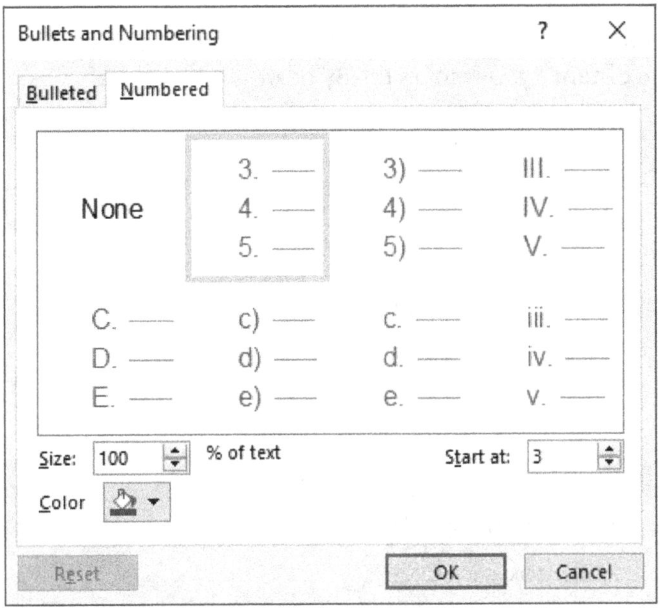

PowerPoint numbered lists must use one of the seven built-in styles

4. Click **OK** to close the dialog box and apply the numbering change.

To demote a list item

→ Click in or select the list item. Then on the **Home** tab, in the **Paragraph** group, click the **Increase List Level** button.

→ Click to the left of the text of the bullet point, and then press the **Tab** key.

To promote a list item

→ Click in or select the list item. Then on the **Home** tab, in the **Paragraph** group, click the **Decrease List Level** button.

→ Click to the left of the text of the bullet point, and then press **Shift+Tab**.

To adjust the hanging indent of a list

1. Select the list items you want to change.

2. On the ruler, drag the **First Line Indent** and **Hanging Indent** markers to the left or right.

Tip To display the ruler, select the Ruler check box in the Show group on the View tab.

Or

1. Select the list items you want to change.

2. Open the **Paragraph** dialog box.

3. In the **Indentation** section, with *Hanging* selected in the **Special** list, enter or select the indent distance you want in the **By** box.

Before Text and Hanging indents for first-level list items match

4. In the **Paragraph** dialog box, click **OK**.

To convert a bulleted or numbered list to regular paragraphs

1. Select the list items.

2. On the **Home** tab, in the **Paragraph** group, click the active **Bullets** or **Numbering** button.

Format text in columns

When a slide includes several short entries, you can balance the slide content and make it easier to read by formatting it in multiple columns. Some slide layouts include text placeholders for multiple columns of text. However, you can format text within any placeholder into multiple columns.

Fit more items on a slide by using columns

The width of the columns is determined by the width of the text placeholder, the number of columns, and the spacing between the columns. You can format text into one, two, or three columns spaced a half inch apart by selecting the number of columns from a list, or you can format text into up to 16 columns by specifying the number and spacing of the columns in the Columns dialog box.

Column formatting options

To format selected text in columns

→ On the **Home** tab, in the **Paragraph** group, click the **Add or Remove Columns** button, and then click **One Column**, **Two Columns**, or **Three Columns**.

Or

1. On the **Home** tab, in the **Paragraph** group, click the **Add or Remove Columns** button, and then click **More Columns**.

2. In the **Columns** dialog box, specify the number of columns and the spacing between the columns, and then click **OK**.

Link to internal and external locations and files

Presentations that are intended to be viewed electronically often include hyperlinks to provide access to supporting information. That information might be on a hidden slide, in another presentation, in a file on your computer or your organization's network, or on a website. If you use Microsoft Outlook, you can also use a hyperlink to open an email message window so that people viewing the presentation can easily contact you.

You can attach a hyperlink to any selected object, such as text, a graphic, a shape, or a table. Clicking the hyperlinked object then takes you directly to the linked location. Editing the object does not disrupt the hyperlink; however, deleting the object also deletes the hyperlink.

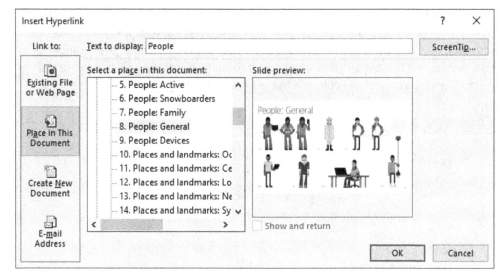

Jump directly to any other slide by using a hyperlink

Tip While inserting a hyperlink from text (not an object), the Text To Display box is active and displays the selected text. (Otherwise, it is unavailable and displays <<*Selection in Document*>>.) You can change the text on the slide by entering alternative text in the box.

To open the Insert Hyperlink dialog box

1. Select the text or object you want to link from.

2. Do any of the following:

    *   On the **Insert** tab, in the **Links** group, click the **Hyperlink** button.

    *   Right-click the selection, and then click **Hyperlink**.

    *   Press **Ctrl+K**.

To create a hyperlink to a slide

1. Open the **Insert Hyperlink** dialog box.

2. In the **Link to** area, click **Place in This Document**.

3. In the **Select a place in this document** list, click the slide you want, and then click **OK**.

To create a hyperlink to a file

1. Open the **Insert Hyperlink** dialog box, and click **Existing File or Web Page** in the **Link to** area.

2. Do either of the following, and then click **OK**:

    *   With **Current Folder** selected, locate and click the file you want.

    *   Click **Recent Files** and then, in the list, click the file you want.

To create a hyperlink to a webpage

1. Open the **Insert Hyperlink** dialog box, and click **Existing File or Web Page** in the **Link to** area.

2. Do either of the following, and then click **OK:**
    *   In the **Address** box, enter the URL of the webpage.
    *   Click **Browsed Pages** and then, in the list, click the URL you want.

To create a hyperlink that creates a pre-addressed email message form

1. Open the **Insert Hyperlink** dialog box, and click **E-mail Address** in the **Link to** area.

2. In the **E-mail address** box, enter the recipient's address.

3. If you want PowerPoint to automatically populate the **Subject** field of any email message created by clicking the hyperlink, enter the subject in the **Subject** box.

4. Click **OK.**

Tip To test a hyperlink, you must be in Slide Show view or Reading view.

To display alternative text when a user points to a hyperlink

1. In the **Insert Hyperlink** dialog box for the link, click the **ScreenTip** button.

2. In the **Set Hyperlink ScreenTip** box, enter the text you want the ScreenTip to display. Then click **OK.**

Set Hyperlink ScreenTip	?	X
ScreenTip text:		
Click to jump to related content		
	OK	Cancel

If you don't customize the ScreenTip, it displays the hyperlink destination and usage instructions

To edit a hyperlink

1. Do either of the following:
    *   Right-click the hyperlinked text or object, and then click **Edit Hyperlink.**
    *   Select the hyperlinked text or object. Then on the **Insert** tab, in the **Links** group, click the **Hyperlink** button.

2. In the **Edit Hyperlink** dialog box, modify any aspect of the hyperlink. Then click **OK.**

To remove a hyperlink

→ Right-click the hyperlink, and then click **Remove Hyperlink.**

→ Open the **Edit Hyperlink** dialog box, click **Remove Link**, and then click **OK.**

Objective 2.1 practice tasks

The practice file for these tasks is located in the **MOSPowerPoint2016 \Objective2** practice file folder. The folder also contains a result file that you can use to check your work.

➤ Open the **PowerPoint_2-1** presentation and do the following:

- ❑ On slide 1, apply the third built-in WordArt style (*Fill: Lime, Accent color 2; Outline: Lime, Accent color 2*) to the presentation title.
- ❑ On slide 2, format the slide title as Bold, Purple (Accent 4), and Small Caps. Set the character spacing to Expanded. Then use the Format Painter to apply the same formatting to the titles of slides 3 through 8.

➤ Return to slide 2 and do the following:

- ❑ Convert the bulleted list items to normal paragraphs.
- ❑ Format the paragraphs in two columns, and then resize the placeholder so the columns are of equal length.
- ❑ Create hyperlinks from each of the following paragraphs to the corresponding slide in the presentation:
  - ○ Preparing for a buying trip
  - ○ Traveling internationally
  - ○ Meeting the client
  - ○ Choosing the merchandise
  - ○ Closing the deal
- ❑ Edit the *Meeting the client* hyperlink to display the ScreenTip <u>How to comport yourself</u>.

➤ Display slide 3 and do the following:

- ❑ Change the first-level bullets to green dollar signs.
- ❑ Increase the hanging indent of the second-level list items to <u>0.5"</u>.

➤ Display slide 8 and do the following:

- ❑ Change the second-level list to a numbered list.
- ❑ Change the numbers to purple capital letters.

➤ Save the **PowerPoint_2-1** presentation.

➤ Open the **PowerPoint_2-1_results** presentation. Compare the two presentations to check your work.

➤ Close the open presentations.

Objective 2.2:
Insert and format shapes and text boxes

Shapes and text boxes are very similar elements—both are text containers. You can format the appearance of the containers and of the text.

Insert and manage text containers

Text boxes are rectangular containers in which you can insert text. They don't, by default, have an outline or shading and so are essentially invisible other than the text they contain. Shapes are text boxes that have a visual overlay identified by the outline and fill. You can create many different types of shapes, including stars, banners, boxes, circles, squares, and clouds. To emphasize, illustrate, or embellish key points in a presentation, you can add simple shapes or complex arrangements of shapes to slides.

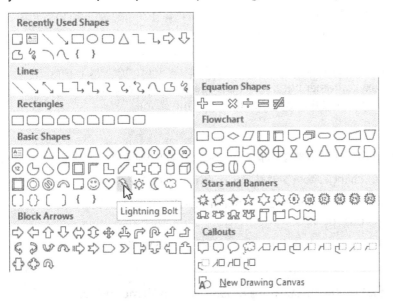

Over 150 shapes are available as starting points for a custom shape

See Also If the simple shapes that are available don't quite fit your needs, you can draw multiple shapes and group them to create a cartoon-like image. For information about grouping and ordering shapes, see "Objective 2.4: Order and group objects."

After you insert a text box or shape on a slide, or if you select one of these objects by clicking it, the object is surrounded by a set of handles. You can change the dimensions, aspect ratio, or rotation of the object by dragging the handles.

For shapes, you can also adjust angles within the shape.

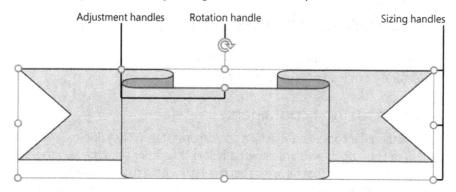

Text boxes have sizing and rotation handles; shapes also have angle-adjustment handles

PowerPoint handles the insertion of text in text boxes and shapes slightly differently:

- When you enter text in a text box, PowerPoint left-aligns the text and expands the container as necessary to hold it.
- When you add text to a shape, PowerPoint centers the text in the text container, which starts out the size of the shape body. If you enter more text, PowerPoint expands the text container but doesn't change the shape size, so overflow text simply expands beyond the top and bottom of the shape.

To insert a text box

1. On the **Insert** tab, in the **Text** group, click the **Text Box** button.

2. After the cursor changes to a plus sign, do either of the following:

    - Click anywhere on the slide to insert a single-character text box that expands as you type in it.
    - Drag to draw a text box of the approximate size that you want.

To insert a shape

1. On the **Insert** tab, in the **Illustrations** group, click the **Shapes** button.

2. In the **Shapes** gallery, click the shape you want, and then do one of the following:

    - Click on the slide to insert a shape of the default dimensions.
    - Drag on the slide to insert a shape of a custom size and shape.

Tip To draw a circle or a square, click the Oval or a Rectangle shape, and hold down the Shift key while you drag.

To add text to a text box or shape

→ Select the container or click in it, and then enter the text.

→ Right-click the container, click **Add Text** or **Edit Text**, and then enter the text.

To change the angles of a selected shape

→ Drag the yellow adjustment handle or handles to change the internal dimensions of the shape without changing its size.

To change the vertices of a selected shape

1. On the **Format** tool tab, in the **Insert Shapes** group, click the **Edit Shape** button, and then click **Edit Points**.

2. Drag the black intersection markers that appear on the shape to change specific vertices, or drag anywhere on the shape border.

To replace a shape with another

1. Select the shape.

2. On the **Format** tool tab, in the **Insert Shapes** group, click **Edit Shape**, click **Change Shape**, and then click the shape you want. The replacement shape retains the formatting and text content of the original shape.

Format text containers

You use the commands in the Shape Styles group on the Format tool tab to format text boxes and shapes. You can choose from built-in styles that combine outline and fill formatting from the presentation color scheme, or you can individually format fill colors, borders, shadows, and other effects.

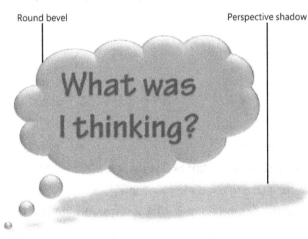

Use built-in effect combinations or create your own

You can modify the appearance of the text within the containers by using standard font formatting techniques (commands in the Font and Paragraph groups on the Home tab and on the Mini Toolbar) and the WordArt styles and text formatting available on the Format tool tab.

Tip Having made changes to one shape or text box, you can easily apply the same attributes to another by using the Format Painter tool.

To modify the dimensions of the selected text container

→ Drag the sizing handles. Guides appear on the slide to indicate alignment with other slide elements.

→ On the **Format** tool tab, in the **Size** group, enter or select dimensions in the **Height** and **Width** boxes.

→ Select the shape to activate the handles, and then do any of the following:

- Drag the white sizing handles to change the external dimensions of the shape.
- Drag the rotating handle to adjust the angle of rotation of the shape.

To rotate the selected text container

→ To rotate the container freely, drag the rotation handle.

→ To rotate the container in 15-degree increments, hold down the **Shift** key and drag the rotation handle.

→ To rotate the container in 90-degree increments, do the following:

a. On the **Format** tool tab, in the **Arrange** group, click **Rotate**.

You can rotate objects or flip them to create mirror images

b. On the **Rotate** menu, click **Rotate Right 90°** or **Rotate Left 90°**.

→ To rotate the container to a specific angle, do the following:

a. On the **Format** tool tab, in the **Arrange** group, click **Rotate**, and then click **More Rotation Options**.

b. In the **Format Shape** pane, in the **Rotation** box, enter or select the angle of rotation you want.

Format Shape

Shape Options   Text Options

▲ Size

Height	0.4"
Width	2.86"
Rotation	37°
Scale Height	100%
Scale Width	100%

☐ Lock aspect ratio

Relative to original picture size

Best scale for slide show

Resolution   640 x 480

▷ **Position**

▷ **Text Box**

▷ **Alt Text**

Set a precise angle of rotation from the Rotate menu

To flip the selected text container

1. On the **Format** tool tab, in the **Arrange** group, click **Rotate**.

2. On the **Rotate** menu, click **Flip Vertical** or **Flip Horizontal**.

To apply a built-in style to the selected text container

→ On the **Format** tool tab, in the **Shape Styles** group, select a preconfigured combination of fill, border, and effects from the **Shape Styles** gallery.

To modify the fill color of the selected text container

→ On the **Format** tool tab, in the **Shape Styles** group, click the **Shape Fill** arrow, and then do one of the following:

- To add or change a fill color, click the color you want, or to remove all color, click **No Fill**.

- To use a color that isn't one of the theme colors, click **More Fill Colors**, and then either click the color that you want on the **Standard** tab, or mix your own color on the **Custom** tab. Custom colors and colors on the Standard tab do not update if you later change the document theme.

- To adjust the transparency of the fill, click **More Fill Colors**. At the bottom of the **Colors** dialog box, move the **Transparency** slider, or enter a number in the box next to the slider. You can vary the percentage of transparency from **0%** (fully opaque, the default setting) to **100%** (fully transparent).

- To choose or change a fill gradient, click **Gradient**, and then click the gradient variation you want. To customize the gradient, click **More Gradients** and then, in the **Format Shape** pane, choose the options you want.

To fill the selected text container with an image or texture

→ On the **Format** tool tab, in the **Shape Styles** group, click the **Shape Fill** arrow, and then do one of the following:

- To choose or change a fill picture, on the **Insert** tab, click **Pictures**. In the **Insert Picture** dialog box, locate the folder that contains the picture that you want to use, click the picture file, and then click **Insert**.

- To choose or change a fill texture, click **Texture**, and then click the texture you want. To customize the texture, click **More Textures** and then, in the **Format Shape** pane, choose the options that you want.

To modify the outline of the selected text container

→ On the **Format** tool tab, in the **Shape Styles** group, click the **Shape Outline** arrow, and then select the outline color, weight, style, and endpoints.

To apply or modify the visual effects of the selected text container

→ On the **Format** tool tab, in the **Shape Styles** group, click the **Shape Effects** arrow, and then select the shadow, reflection, glow, soft edge, beveled edge, and rotation effects you want.

To format text in a selected shape

→ On the **Format** tool tab, in the **WordArt Styles** group, click the **More** button to expand the **WordArt** gallery and then, in the **WordArt** gallery, click the text style you want.

→ On the **Format** tool tab, in the **WordArt Styles** group, click the **Text Fill**, **Text Outline**, or **Text Effects** arrow, and then select the individual formatting options you want.

→ On the **Home** tab, in the **Font** group, use the commands to set the font, font size, and font formatting options you want.

→ On the **Home** tab, in the **Paragraph** group, use the commands to modify the text alignment, spacing, and direction.

To apply the attributes of a shape to all future shapes in the active presentation

→ Right-click the shape, and then click **Set as Default Shape**.

Objective 2.2 practice tasks

The practice file for these tasks is located in the **MOSPowerPoint2016 \Objective2** practice file folder. The folder also contains a result file that you can use to check your work.

➤ Open the **PowerPoint_2-2** presentation and do the following on slide 1:

☐ Insert Sun, Moon, and Heart shapes at their default sizes.

☐ Set the Sun shape to a size of <u>3"</u> by <u>3"</u>, the Moon shape to a size of <u>2"</u> by <u>1.5"</u>, and the Heart shape to a size of <u>2"</u> by <u>2"</u>.

☐ Rotate the Moon shape by 180 degrees so that the open curve is on the left and the outer curve is on the right.

☐ Select the three shapes, and then apply a 1-point, White outline.

☐ Using the colors from the Standard Colors palette, fill the Sun shape with Yellow, the Moon shape with Orange, and the Heart shape with Red.

☐ Add the word <u>Nature</u> to the Sun shape, the word <u>Sleep</u> to the Moon shape, and the word <u>Family</u> to the Heart shape. Then format the words by applying the first WordArt Quick Style (*Fill – Black, Text 1, Shadow*).

☐ Flip the Moon shape vertically so that its text is right-side up. Then rotate the text 270 degrees so that the text runs sideways from bottom to top.

➤ Save the **PowerPoint_2-2** presentation.

➤ Open the **PowerPoint_2-2_results** presentation. Compare the two presentations to check your work.

➤ Close the open presentations.

Objective 2.3: Insert and format images

Insert images

You can insert digital photographs or pictures created in almost any program into a PowerPoint presentation. Image sources include the following:

- Local images that are saved as files on your computer, on a network drive, or on a device (such as a digital camera) that is connected to your computer.

- Online images that are saved in your Facebook or Flickr account storage or on your OneDrive.

- Online images that are available through a web search. Many images can be reused for private or limited commercial purposes under the Creative Commons media licensing. Other images located through a web search might have restricted permissions, so it's important to be careful when reusing an online image in a document.

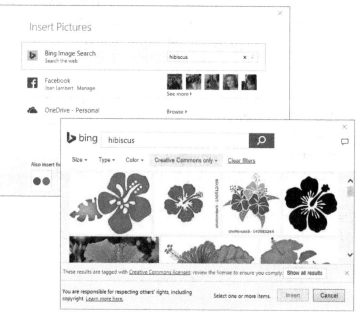

Search the web from within Word for images that you can insert in a document

Exam Strategy Capturing and inserting images by using the screen clipping tool is beyond the scope of MOS Exam 77-729: PowerPoint 2016: Core Presentation Design and Delivery Skills.

To insert an image from a file

1. In a content placeholder, or in the **Images** group on the **Insert** tab, click the **Pictures** button.

2. In the **Insert Picture** dialog box, browse to and click the file you want. Then do one of the following:

   - Click **Insert** to insert the image on the slide.
   - In the **Insert** list, click **Link to File** to insert an image that will update automatically if the image file changes.
   - In the **Insert** list, click **Insert and Link** to insert an image that you can manually update if the image file changes.

To insert an online image

1. In a content placeholder, or in the **Images** group on the **Insert** tab, click the **Online Pictures** button.
2. In the **Insert Pictures** window, click the online source (Bing Image Search, a Microsoft SharePoint site or OneDrive folder, or one of the available linked third-party sites).
3. Enter a keyword in the search box and press **Enter**, or navigate to the picture you want to insert.
4. Double-click the image you want to insert.

Tip You change the size, shape, layout, and location of images by using the same techniques that you use with other graphic elements and in other Office 2016 programs.

Format images

After you insert an image on a slide, you can modify it in many ways. For example, you can crop or resize an image, change the image's brightness and contrast, recolor it, and apply artistic effects to it. You can apply a wide range of preformatted styles to an image to change its shape and orientation, and also to add borders and picture effects.

If you want to display only part of the content of an image, you can crop it, or you can make parts of the image transparent by using the Remove Background tool.

Incorporate only the portion of the image that you want

You modify the image by using commands on the Format tool tab for Pictures, which is displayed only when an image is selected.

- The Adjust group contains commands that enable you to change the image's brightness and contrast, recolor it, apply artistic effects to it, and compress it to reduce the size of the presentation.

- The Picture Styles group offers a wide range of picture styles that you can apply to an image to change its shape and orientation, and to add borders and picture effects. This group includes the Quick Styles gallery, which contains many style combinations that you can apply very quickly.

- The Arrange group contains commands for specifying the relationship of the image to the page and to other elements on the page.

- The Size group contains commands for cropping and resizing images.

Changes that you make to images on slides (such as cropping, removing backgrounds, and applying effects) aren't permanent and can be reverted at any time unless you specifically choose to remove cropped content to reduce file size.

To apply a picture frame style to a selected image

→ On the **Format** tool tab, in the **Picture Styles** group, expand the **Quick Styles** gallery, and then click the style you want to apply.

Or

1. On the **Format** tool tab, click the **Picture Styles** dialog box launcher.
2. In the **Format Picture** pane, on the **Fill & Line**, **Effects**, **Layout & Properties**, and **Picture** pages, choose the settings you want to apply. Then click **Close**.

To apply artistic effects to a selected image

1. On the **Format** tool tab, in the **Adjust** group, click the **Artistic Effects** button to display the Artistic Effects gallery.
2. Point to each effect to display a live preview of the effect on the selected photo.

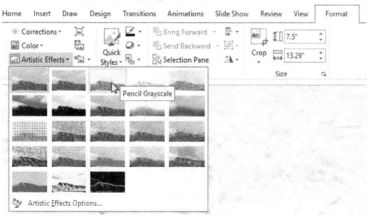

Point to any effect to display a preview on the original picture

3. Click the effect that you want to apply.

To remove background elements from a selected image

1. On the **Format** tool tab, in the **Adjust** group, click the **Remove Background** button to display the Background Removal tool tab and apply purple shading to the areas of the picture that the tool thinks you want to remove.

2. Drag the white handles to define the area that you want to keep. The Background Removal tool updates its shading as you do.

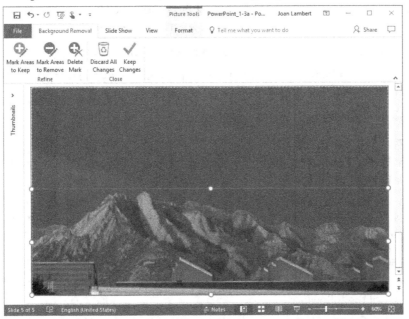

The accuracy of the estimate depends on the intricacy of the background

3. On the **Background Removal** tool tab, click **Mark Areas to Keep**, and then click any areas of the photo that are shaded, that you'd like to expose and keep.

4. On the **Background Removal** tool tab, click **Mark Areas to Remove**, and then click any areas of the photo that aren't shaded, that you'd like to remove. Depending on the simplicity of the picture, you might need to make a lot of adjustments or only a few.

5. When you finish, click the **Keep Changes** button to display the results. You can return to the Background Removal tool tab at any time to make adjustments.

To discard changes made to a selected image

1. On the **Format** tool tab, in the **Adjust** group, click the **Reset Picture** arrow.
2. Do either of the following:
   - Choose **Reset Picture** to discard formatting changes only.
   - Choose **Reset Picture & Size** to discard all formatting and size changes.

To apply picture effects to a selected image

→ On the **Format** tool tab, in the **Picture Styles** group, click **Picture Effects**, point to any category to expand the gallery, and then click the effect you want to apply.

To change the brightness, contrast, or color of a selected image

→ In the **Format Picture** pane, on the **Picture** page, modify the settings in the **Picture Corrections** and **Picture Color** sections.

To change the size or shape of a selected image

→ Drag its sizing handles.
→ On the **Format** tool tab, in the **Size** group, change the **Shape Height** and **Shape Width** settings.
→ On the **Format** tool tab, click the **Size** dialog box launcher. Then on the **Size & Properties** page of the **Format Picture** pane, change the **Height**, **Width**, or **Scale** settings.

To crop a selected image

→ On the **Format** tool tab, in the **Size** group, click the **Crop** arrow, and then do either of the following:
   - Click **Crop to Shape** to display the menu of more than 150 available shapes, and then click a shape.
   - Click **Aspect Ratio**, and then in the **Square**, **Portrait**, or **Landscape** section of the menu, click an aspect ratio.

Or

1. On the **Format** tool tab, in the **Size** group, click the **Crop** button to display thick black handles on the sides and in the corners of the picture.
2. Drag the handles to define the area you want to crop to. The areas that will be cropped from the picture are shaded.

> **Tip** The crop handles and sizing handles are close to each other; take care to not drag the wrong handle.

3. When you finish defining the crop area, click away from the picture or click the **Crop** button again to apply the crop effect.

> **Tip** To redisplay the original version of a cropped image, select it and click the Crop button.

Objective 2.3 practice tasks

The practice files for these tasks are located in the **MOSPowerPoint2016 \Objective2** practice file folder. The folder also contains a result file that you can use to check your work.

➤ Open the **PowerPoint_2-3a** presentation and do the following on slide 4:

❑ From the practice file folder, insert the **PowerPoint_2-3b** image of skiers.

❑ Maintaining the aspect ratio, set the height of the image to <u>4</u>″.

❑ Position the image in the lower-right corner of the slide.

❑ Remove the background from the image to isolate the skiers.

❑ Apply the *Photocopy* artistic effect to the picture.

❑ Apply the *Drop Shadow Rectangle* picture style to the picture. Notice that the drop shadow applies to the skiers rather than to the original picture frame.

➤ Save the **PowerPoint_2-3a** presentation.

➤ Open the **PowerPoint_2-3_results** presentation. Compare the two presentations to check your work.

➤ Close the open presentations.

Objective 2.4: Order and group objects

PowerPoint alignment tools

PowerPoint 2016 has several tools that help you to arrange content on a slide or slide master:

- The horizontal and vertical rulers measure the distance from the center of a slide.
- Gridlines are fixed indicators that mark a grid of the size you select by using major and minor indicators. The default gridlines mark off half-inch squares, with indicators every 1/12 inch. You can have PowerPoint snap objects to the grid regardless of whether the grid is currently displayed.
- Guides are movable indicators that help you to align objects with other objects.
- Smart guides appear when the object you're moving is aligned with the edge or centerline of another object, is equidistant from two points, or reflects the spacing of a parallel object.

A variety of alignment tools are available if you need them

IMPORTANT You can turn on and off the display of the alignment tools only when the presentation is in Normal view or Outline view.

To display or hide rulers

➜ On the **View** tab, in the **Show** group, select or clear the **Ruler** check box.

➜ Press **Shift+Alt+F9**.

To display or hide gridlines

➜ On the **View** tab, in the **Show** group, select or clear the **Gridlines** check box.

➜ Press **Shift+F9**.

To manage gridlines and guidelines

1. On the **View** tab, click the **Show** dialog box launcher.

2. In the **Grid and Guides** dialog box, select the check boxes of the features you want to turn on.

Configure the grid to meet your needs

3. In the **Spacing** list, select standard grid spacing from **1/24"** to **2"**, or click **Custom**, enter specific spacing in the adjacent box, and then click **OK**.

Align objects

After inserting pictures or drawing shapes in the approximate locations you want them on a slide, you can align them to provide a sense of order and balance. You can use the automatic alignment commands to align individual or multiple graphics in several ways. For example, you can:

■ Align objects with each other horizontally or vertically by any edge or centerline

■ Distribute graphics evenly within their current space, either horizontally or vertically.

■ Align objects relative to the slide that contains them or to other selected objects.

The simplest way to align objects is by using the smart guides that appear when you drag objects on the slide.

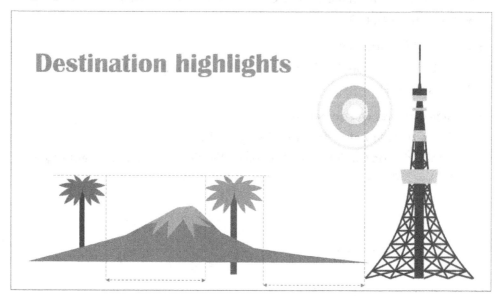

Smart guides appear as dashed lines that indicate the alignment and spacing of objects

---

Tip Smart guides are turned on by default. If you would prefer that they not appear, turn them off by clearing the Display Smart Guides When Shapes Are Aligned check box in the Grid And Guides dialog box.

If you prefer not to depend on the smart guides, you can use the tools on the Format tool tab to specifically align and distribute objects.

To align objects with the slide

1. On the slide or in the **Selection** pane, select one or more objects that you want to align with the slide.
2. On the **Format** tool tab, in the **Arrange** group, click the **Align** button.
3. On the **Align** menu, if the **Align to Slide** option is not selected, click that option. Then click **Align Left**, **Align Center**, **Align Right**, **Align Top**, **Align Middle**, or **Align Bottom**.

To align objects with other objects

→ With the smart guides feature turned on, drag a shape until the smart guide indicates that it is aligned with another.

Or

1. Select two or more objects you want to align with each other.
2. On the **Format** tool tab, in the **Arrange** group, click the **Align** button.
3. On the **Align** menu, with the **Align Selected Objects** options selected, click **Align Left**, **Align Center**, **Align Right**, **Align Top**, **Align Middle**, or **Align Bottom**.

To distribute shapes evenly within the current container

1. Select three or more shapes you want to distribute.
2. On the **Align** menu, click **Distribute Horizontally** or **Distribute Vertically**.

Stack and reorder objects

When multiple objects exist on the same space on a slide, the stacking order of the objects determines which objects obscure others.

Regardless of whether graphics and other slide elements actually overlap each other, all the elements on an individual slide are stacked in a specific order. The default stacking order is determined by the order in which elements are inserted. Opaque elements (such as graphics, filled shapes, and filled text boxes) that are later in the stacking order can hide elements that are earlier in the stacking order.

You can change the stacking order by moving objects forward and backward or by specifying the order in the Selection pane.

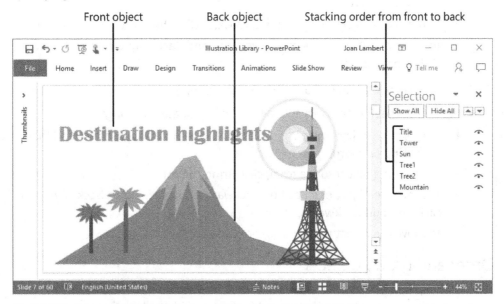

The Selection pane provides a convenient way of selecting and ordering objects

---

Tip If you can't select an object on a slide because it is covered by another, select and reorder the object from within the Selection pane. PowerPoint assigns names to objects on the slide; you can change the default names to more descriptive names.

To display the Selection pane

➜ On the **Home** tab, in the **Editing** group, click **Select**, and then click **Selection Pane**.

➜ On the **Format** tool tab, in the **Arrange** group, click **Selection Pane**.

To change the stacking order of objects from within the Selection pane

1. On the slide or in the **Selection** pane, select the object that you want to move in the stacking order.

2. In the **Selection** pane, do any of the following:

   • To move the object one position forward, click the **Bring Forward** button (the up arrow).

   • To move the object one position backward, click the **Send Backward** button (the down arrow).

   • Drag the selected object to any position in the order.

To change the stacking order of objects from the ribbon

➜ On the **Format** tool tab, in the **Arrange** group, do any of the following:

   • To move the object one position forward, click the **Bring Forward** button.

   • To move the object to the front, click the **Bring Forward** arrow, and then click **Bring to Front**.

   • To move the object one position backward, click the **Send Backward** button.

   • To move the object to the back, click the **Send Backward** arrow, and then click **Send to Back**.

To change the stacking order of objects from the slide

➜ Right-click the selected object, and then do any of the following:

   • To move the object one position forward, point to **Bring to Front**, and then click **Bring Forward**.

   • To move the object to the front, click **Bring to Front**.

   • To move the object one position backward, point to **Send to Back**, and then click the **Send Backward** button.

   • To move the object to the back, click **Send to Back**.

Order and group objects

You can group multiple objects on a slide so that you can copy, move, and format them as a unit. You can change the attributes of an individual object in the group— for example, you can change the color or size of a shape—without ungrouping the objects. If you do ungroup them, you can easily regroup the same selection of objects.

In the Selection pane, grouped objects appear under a common heading.

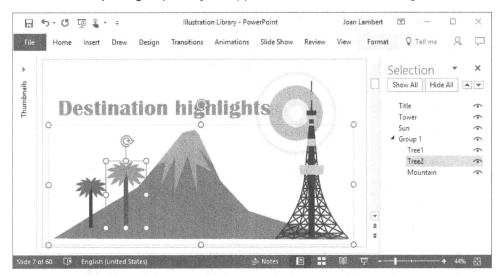

Selecting a grouped object displays the object handles and the group handles

To group objects

1. Select two or more objects that you want to group.
2. Do either of the following:
    - On the **Format** tool tab, in the **Arrange** group, click the **Group Objects** button, and then click **Group**.
    - Right-click the selection, click **Group**, and then click **Group**.

To ungroup objects

1. Select a group by clicking any object in the group and then clicking the outer selection outline.
2. Do either of the following:
    - On the **Format** tool tab, in the **Arrange** group, click the **Group Objects** button, and then click **Ungroup**.
    - Right-click the selection, click **Group**, and then click **Ungroup**.

To regroup objects

1. Select one object from the original group.
2. Do either of the following:
    - On the **Format** tool tab, in the **Arrange** group, click the **Group Objects** button, and then click **Regroup**.
    - Right-click the selection, click **Group**, and then click **Regroup**.

Objective 2.4 practice tasks

The practice file for these tasks is located in the **MOSPowerPoint2016 \Objective2** practice file folder. The folder also contains a result file that you can use to check your work.

➤ Open the **PowerPoint_2-4** presentation and do the following:

- ❑ Select the three shapes on the slide, and align them all with the middle and center of the slide.
- ❑ Change the stacking order so that the Heart is in front, the Sun second, the Moon third, and the slide title in back.
- ❑ Distribute the three shapes horizontally on the slide.
- ❑ Group the three shapes.

➤ Save the **PowerPoint_2-4** presentation.

➤ Open the **PowerPoint_2-4_results** presentation. Compare the two presentations to check your work.

➤ Close the open presentations.

Objective group 3

Insert tables, charts, SmartArt, and media

The skills tested in this section of the Microsoft Office Specialist exam for Microsoft PowerPoint 2016 relate to inserting and formatting tables, charts, and SmartArt graphics, and inserting and managing media. Specifically, the following objectives are associated with this set of skills:

- **3.1** Insert and format tables
- **3.2** Insert and format charts
- **3.3** Insert and format SmartArt graphics
- **3.4** Insert and manage media

Many PowerPoint users take slide content "beyond bullet points" and express information by using imagery. PowerPoint 2016 has many ways of expressing information visually. You can display numeric data in tables or summarize it in charts, express the flow of a process by using SmartArt business graphics, or embed supplementary videos directly onto a slide. You can also embed audio recordings to provide a soundtrack or special effects. All these methods help to keep a presentation engaging and informative.

This chapter guides you in studying ways of inserting tables, charts, and SmartArt graphics, audio clips, and video clips on slides; formatting tables, charts, and graphics; and managing media elements.

3

To complete the practice tasks in this chapter, you need the practice files contained in the **MOSPowerPoint2016\Objective3** practice file folder. For more information, see "Download the practice files" in this book's introduction.

Objective 3.1: Insert and format tables

Create and import tables

When you want to present a lot of data in an organized and easy-to-read format, a table is often your best choice. You can create a table in one of the following ways:

- Have PowerPoint insert a table with the number of columns and rows you specify.
- Draw the table by dragging on the slide to create cells that are the size and shape you need.
- If the table already exists in a Microsoft Word document, Excel workbook, Outlook email message, or another PowerPoint slide, you can copy the original table and paste it onto a slide rather than re-create it.

If you want to use data from an Excel worksheet in a PowerPoint table, you can do any of the following:

- Copy and paste the data as a table.
- Embed the worksheet on a slide as an object.
- Link the slide to the worksheet so that the slide reflects any changes you make to the worksheet data.

SCHEDULE

Project	Training Date	Teaching Date
American Symbols	October 10	October 20
Revolutionary Pop Prints	December 5	December 8
Lewis & Clark Animal Sketch	January 30	February 9
Civil War Quilt	February 27	March 10
Tiffany Lamp	March 27	April 19

Tables display information in rows and columns

To enter information in a table, you simply click a cell and then enter text. You can also move the cursor from cell to cell by pressing the Tab key.

To create a new table

1. In a content placeholder, click the **Insert Table** button.
2. In the **Insert Table** dialog box, specify the number of columns and rows, and then click **OK**.

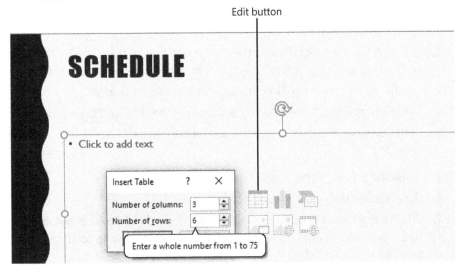

Some content placeholders include table options

3. Enter or copy and paste the information into the table structure.

Or

1. On the **Insert** tab, in the **Tables** group, click the **Table** button.
2. Move the pointer across and down the grid to select the number of columns and rows you want, and then click the lower-right cell in the selection.
3. Enter or copy and paste the information into the table structure.

To insert a table from Word

1. In the source document, click the table border to select it.
2. Copy the table to the Microsoft Office Clipboard.
3. Switch to PowerPoint, display the destination slide, and then paste the table from the Clipboard.

To paste Excel data as a table

1. In the Excel worksheet, select and copy the data you want to display in the PowerPoint table.
2. Switch to PowerPoint, display the destination slide, and then paste the data.
3. To change the default paste option (Use Destination Styles), click the **Paste Options** button, and then click the option you want.

To embed an editable worksheet

1. In the Excel worksheet, select and copy the data you want to display on the PowerPoint slide.

2. Switch to PowerPoint, display the destination slide, click the **Paste Options** button, and then click **Embed**.

Or

1. In the workbook that contains the worksheet, ensure that the worksheet you want to embed is the active worksheet, and then save and close the workbook.

2. On the **Insert** tab, in the **Text** group, click the **Object** button.

3. In the **Insert Object** dialog box, click **Create from file**, and then click **Browse**.

4. In the **Browse** dialog box, locate and double-click the workbook, and then click **OK**.

To hide unused columns and rows

1. Double-click the worksheet object.

2. When the worksheet opens in an Excel window within PowerPoint, size the frame around the worksheet so that it is just big enough to contain the active part of the worksheet.

3. Click outside the frame to return to PowerPoint.

To resize the worksheet

→ Point to any handle (the sets of dots) around the worksheet object, and then drag to enlarge or shrink it.

To modify an embedded worksheet

1. Double-click the worksheet object.

2. Use Excel techniques to edit and format the embedded object.

To link to a worksheet

→ Follow the instructions for embedding a worksheet, but in the **Insert Object** dialog box, select the **Link** check box before clicking **OK**.

To update a linked worksheet

→ Double-click the table on the slide to open the linked worksheet in Excel, make the changes, and then save them.

→ If you update the linked worksheet in Excel and want to synchronize the table on the slide, right-click the table on the slide, and then click **Update Link**.

To update table data

→ Use normal editing techniques to change the data in a cell.

To delete a table

→ On the **Layout** tool tab, in the **Rows & Columns** group, click the **Delete** button, and then click **Delete Table**.

Change table structure

When a table is selected, the Design and Layout tool tabs are available on the ribbon.

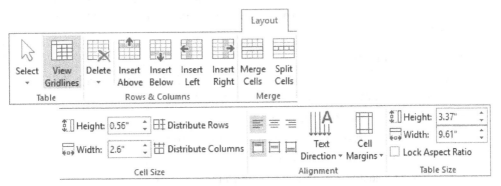

PowerPoint has most of the same table layout tools as Word

After you insert a table, you can change its structure in the following ways:

- Add columns or rows.
- Delete columns or rows.
- Combine (merge) selected cells into one cell that spans two or more columns or rows.
- Split a single cell into two or more cells.
- Resize individual columns or rows, or the whole table.

	Project	Training Date	Teaching Date
1	American Symbols	October 10	October 20
2	Revolutionary Pop Prints	December 5	December 8
3	Lewis & Clark Animal Sketch	January 30	February 9
4	Civil War Quilt	February 27	March 10
5	Tiffany Lamp	March 27	April 19

The Project heading is in a merged cell at the top of the first two columns

To insert a row

→ In the last cell of the last row, press **Tab** to insert a row at the end of the table.

→ On the **Layout** tool tab, in the **Rows & Columns** group, click the **Insert Above** or **Insert Below** button to insert a row above or below the row containing the cursor.

To insert a column

➔ On the **Layout** tool tab, in the **Rows & Columns** group, click the **Insert Left** or **Insert Right** button to insert a column to the left or right of the column containing the cursor.

To delete a row or column

➔ On the **Layout** tool tab, in the **Rows & Columns** group, click the **Delete** button, and then click **Delete Columns** or **Delete Rows** to delete the row or column containing the cursor.

To select table elements

➔ To select a cell, point just inside its left border, and then click when the cursor changes to a black arrow pointing up and to the right.

➔ To select a column, do either of the following:

- Point above its top border, and then click when the cursor changes to a black downward-pointing arrow.
- Drag to select all the cells in the column.
- Click a cell in the column, and on the **Layout** tool tab, in the **Table** group, click the **Select** button, and then click **Select Column**.

➔ To select a row, do either of the following:

- Point outside the table to the left of the row, and then click when the cursor changes to a black right-pointing arrow.
- Drag to select all the cells in the row.
- Click a cell in the row, and on the **Layout** tool tab, in the **Table** group, click the **Select** button, and then click **Select Row**.

➔ To select multiple cells, columns, or rows, do either of the following:

- Select the first element, and then hold down the **Shift** key as you select subsequent elements.
- Drag through adjacent cells, columns, or rows.

➔ To select an entire table, click any cell, and on the **Layout** tool tab, in the **Table** group, click the **Select** button, and then click **Select Table**.

To split one or more cells

1. Select the cell or contiguous cells that you want to split.
2. Do either of the following to open the Split Cells dialog box:
   - On the **Layout** tool tab, in the **Merge** group, click the **Split Cells** button.
   - Right-click the selection, and then click **Split Cells**.

3. In the **Split Cells** dialog box, specify the number of columns and rows you want the cell to be split into, and then click **OK**.

Split Cells	?	X
Number of columns:	2	
Number of rows:	5	
OK	Cancel	

You can reform rows and columns at the same time

To merge two or more selected cells in a row or column

→ On the **Layout** tool tab, in the **Merge** group, click the **Merge Cells** button.

→ Right-click the selection, and then click **Merge Cells**.

To change the size of a selected element

→ To change the width of a column, do either of the following:

- Point to the right border of one of its cells, and when the opposing arrows appear, drag the border to the left or right.

- On the **Layout** tool tab, in the **Cell Size** group, adjust the **Table Column Width** setting.

→ To fit the column to the width of its entries, point to the right border of one of its cells, and when the opposing arrows appear, double-click.

→ To change the height of a row, do either of the following:

- Point to the bottom border of one of its cells, and when the opposing arrows appear, drag the border up or down.

- On the **Layout** tool tab, in the **Cell Size** group, adjust the **Table Row Height** setting.

→ To evenly distribute the widths of selected columns or the heights of selected rows, on the **Layout** tool tab, in the **Cell Size** group, click the **Distribute Columns** or **Distribute Rows** button.

→ To change the size of a selected table, do either of the following:

- Point to any handle (the sets of dots) around its frame, and then drag in the direction you want the table to grow or shrink.

- On the **Layout** tool tab, in the **Table Size** group, adjust the **Height** or **Width** setting.

3

Format tables

You can format the text in a table in the same ways you would format regular text. You can also easily do the following:

- Align text horizontally or vertically within a cell.
- Set the text direction.
- Set the cell margins.
- Apply Quick Styles, fills, outlines, and text effects.

In addition to formatting the text in a table, you can format the table itself in the following ways:

- Apply a ready-made table style.
- Customize the style by setting various options.
- Add shading, borders, and effects such as shadows and reflections to individual cells.

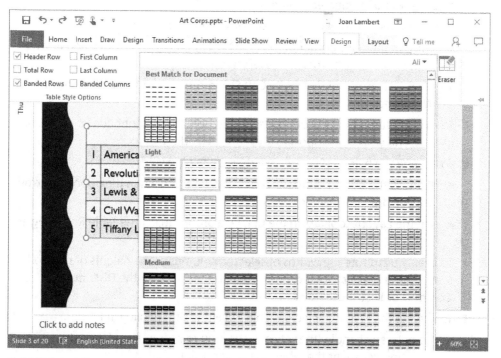

Quick Styles use the presentation theme colors and reflect the current table style option set

To align text

→ On the **Layout** tool tab, in the **Alignment** group, click one of the **Align** buttons.

To set text direction

→ In the **Alignment** group, click the **Text Direction** button, and then click one of the rotation options.

To set cell margins

→ In the **Alignment** group, click the **Cell Margins** button, and then click one of the preset options.

→ In the **Cell Margins** list, click **Custom Margins**, and then in the **Cell Text Layout** dialog box, set specific margins.

To apply a table style

→ On the **Design** tool tab, in the **Table Styles** gallery, click the style you want.

To format selected cells

→ In the **Table Styles** group, click the **Shading**, **Border**, or **Effects** button, and then click the options you want.

To create a custom table style

→ On the **Design** tool tab, in the **Table Style Options** group, select or clear the six check boxes to format the table cells to suit your data.

To apply Quick Styles and other fancy formatting

→ On the **Design** tool tab, in the **WordArt Styles** group, click the **Quick Styles** button, and then click the style you want.

→ In the **WordArt Styles** group, click the **Text Fill**, **Text Outline**, or **Text Effects** button, and then click the options you want in the corresponding galleries.

3

Objective 3.1 practice tasks

The practice file for these tasks is located in the **MOSPowerPoint2016 \Objective3** practice file folder. The folder also contains a result file that you can use to check your work.

➤ Open the **PowerPoint_3-1a** presentation, display slide 2, and do the following:

❑ Insert a table that has three columns and four rows.

❑ In the top row of the table, enter <u>Task</u>, <u>Minutes/Day</u>, and <u>Hours Saved/Week</u>.

❑ Enter the following in the cells of the Task column: <u>Paper documents</u>, <u>Email</u>, and <u>Calendar</u>.

❑ Insert a new row at the top of the table, and merge all the cells in the row. In the merged cell, enter and center the title <u>Effect of Focused Activity</u>.

❑ In the table, turn off Banded Rows formatting, and turn on First Column formatting. Then apply the *Medium Style 2 - Accent 2* style to the table, and apply a border around the entire table.

➤ Display slide 3 and do the following:

❑ Embed the worksheet from the **PowerPoint_3-1b** workbook on the slide.

❑ Enlarge the worksheet object so that it fills the available space on the slide.

➤ Save the **PowerPoint_3-1a** presentation.

➤ Open the **PowerPoint_3-1_results** presentation. Compare the two presentations to check your work.

➤ Close the open presentations.

Objective 3.2: Insert and format charts

Create and import charts

You can easily add a chart to a slide to help identify trends that might not be obvious from looking at numbers. When you create a chart in PowerPoint, you specify the chart type and then use a linked Excel worksheet to enter the information you want to plot. As you replace the sample data in the worksheet with your own data, you immediately see the results in the chart in the adjacent PowerPoint window.

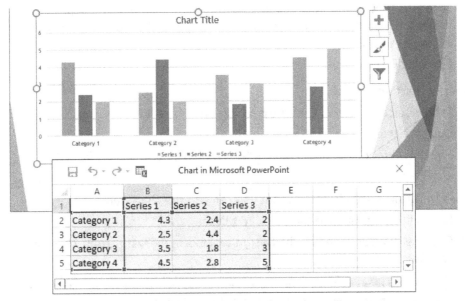

PowerPoint provides a starting point for your chart

You can enter the data directly into the linked worksheet, or you can copy and paste it from an existing Microsoft Access table, Word table, or Excel worksheet. You then identify the chart data range in the linked worksheet to ensure that only the data you want appears in the chart, and close the worksheet to plot the data.

By default, a chart is plotted based on the series of data points in the columns of the attached worksheet, and these series are identified in the legend. You can tell PowerPoint to plot the chart based on the series in the rows instead.

When a chart is active on a slide, the Design, Layout, and Format tool tabs are available on the ribbon.

At any time after you plot data in the chart, you can reopen the attached worksheet and edit the data; PowerPoint updates the chart to reflect your changes.

To create a chart

1. Do either of the following to open the Insert Chart dialog box:
   - In a content placeholder, click the **Insert Chart** button.
   - On the **Insert** tab, in the **Illustrations** group, click the **Chart** button.
2. In the **Insert Chart** dialog box, click a chart category in the left pane, click a chart type in the right pane, and then click **OK**.
3. In the linked Excel worksheet, enter the values to be plotted, following the pattern of the sample data.
4. Ensure that the blue border delineating the chart data range encompasses only the data you want included in the chart, by dragging the blue handle in the lower-right corner of the range.
5. Close the Excel window.

To insert a chart from Excel

1. In the source workbook, click the chart border to select it.
2. Copy the chart to the Clipboard.
3. Switch to PowerPoint, display the slide, and then paste the chart from the Clipboard.

To open the attached worksheet so that you can edit the chart data

→ Right-click the chart, and then click **Edit Data**.
→ Click the chart, and then on the **Design** tool tab, in the **Data** group, click the **Edit Data** button.

Tip The chart must be active (surrounded by a frame) when you make changes to the data in the worksheet; otherwise, the chart won't automatically update.

To plot a selected chart by rows instead of columns

1. Open the chart's attached worksheet.
2. On the **Design** tool tab, in the **Data** group, click the **Switch Row/Column** button.

Tip The Switch Row/Column button is active only when the worksheet is open.

To select worksheet data for editing

→ To select a cell, click it.
→ To select a column, click the column header (the letter at the top of the column).
→ To select a row, click the row header (the number at the left end of the row).

→ To select multiple cells, columns, or rows, do either of the following:

- Select the first element, and then hold down the **Shift** key as you select subsequent elements.
- Drag through adjacent cells, columns, or rows.

→ To select an entire worksheet, click the **Select All** button (the triangle in the upper-left corner of the worksheet, at the intersection of the row and column headers).

Change the chart type, layout, and elements

If you decide that the type of chart you initially selected doesn't adequately depict your data, you can change the type at any time. There are 16 chart categories, each with two-dimensional and three-dimensional variations.

Each chart type has corresponding chart layouts that you can use to refine the look of the chart.

Pointing to any Quick Layout displays a preview of that layout on the current chart

The Quick Layouts are preset combinations of the available chart elements, which include the following:

- **Chart area** This is the entire area within the chart frame.
- **Plot area** This is the rectangle between the horizontal and vertical axes.
- **Data markers** These are the graphical representations of the values, or *data points*, you enter in the Excel worksheet. Sometimes the data markers are identified with data labels.
- **Legend** This provides a key for identifying the *data series* (a set of data points).
- **Axes** The data is plotted against an x-axis—also called the category axis—and a y-axis—also called the *value axis*. (Three-dimensional charts also have a z-axis—also called the *series axis*.) Sometimes the axes are identified with axis labels.
- **Axis labels** These identify the categories, values, or series along each axis.
- **Gridlines** These help to visually quantify the data points.
- **Data table** This table provides details of the plotted data points in table format.
- **Titles** The chart might have a title and subtitle.

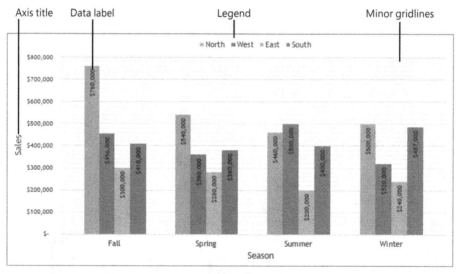

Some of the optional chart elements

When the preset layouts don't produce the chart you want, you can create a custom layout by mixing and matching different chart elements.

You can adjust a chart layout by adding, deleting, moving, and sizing chart elements. To perform any of those tasks, you must first select the element.

If you want more control over the layout of a chart, you can do the following:

- Control the overall size of the chart.
- Adjust the size of chart elements.
- Arrange chart elements precisely.

To change the type of a selected chart

1. On the **Design** tool tab, in the **Type** group, click the **Change Chart Type** button.
2. In the **Change Chart Type** dialog box, click a category on the left, click a chart type at the top, and then click **OK**.

> **Tip** Click a chart type in the top row to preview that chart type as applied to the current data. Point to the preview to display a larger version.

To apply a preset layout to a selected chart

→ On the **Design** tool tab, in the **Chart Layouts** gallery, click the **Quick Layout** button, and then click the layout you want.

To add or remove an axis

→ On the **Design** tool tab, in the **Chart Layouts** group, click the **Add Chart Element** button, click **Axes**, and then click to select **Primary Horizontal**, **Primary Vertical**, or both.

→ Click a selected axis to remove it from the chart.

To add or remove an axis title

→ In the **Chart Layouts** group, click the **Add Chart Element** button, click **Axis Titles**, and then click to select **Primary Horizontal Axis Title**, **Primary Vertical Axis Title**, or both.

→ Click a selected axis title to remove it from the chart.

To add or remove a chart title

→ In the **Chart Layouts** group, click the **Add Chart Element** button, click **Chart Title**, and then click **None**, **Above Chart**, or **Centered Overlay**.

To add or remove data labels

→ In the **Chart Layouts** group, click the **Add Chart Element** button, click **Data Labels**, and then click **None**, **Center**, **Inside End**, **Inside Base**, **Outside End**, or **Data Callout**.

To add or remove a data table

→ In the **Chart Layouts** group, click the **Add Chart Element** button, click **Data Table**, and then click **None**, **With Legend Keys**, or **No Legend Keys**.

3

To add or remove error bars

➜ In the **Chart Layouts** group, click the **Add Chart Element** button, click **Legend**, and then click **None, Standard Error, Percentage**, or **Deviation**.

To add or remove gridlines

➜ In the **Chart Layouts** group, click the **Add Chart Element** button, click **Gridlines**, and then click to select **Primary Major Horizontal, Primary Major Vertical, Primary Minor Horizontal, Primary Minor Vertical**, or any combination of the four options.

➜ Click a selected gridline option to remove it from the chart.

To add or remove a legend

➜ In the **Chart Layouts** group, click the **Add Chart Element** button, click **Legend**, and then click **None, Right, Top, Left**, or **Bottom**.

To add or remove lines (line charts only)

➜ In the **Chart Layouts** group, click the **Add Chart Element** button, click **Lines**, and then click **None, Drop Lines**, or **High-Low Lines**.

To add or remove a trendline (line charts only)

➜ In the **Chart Layouts** group, click the **Add Chart Element** button, click **Trendline**, and then click **None, Linear, Exponential, Linear Forecast**, or **Moving Average**.

Tip You can use standard techniques to add pictures, shapes, and independent text boxes to slides to enhance charts.

To change the size of a selected chart

➜ Point to any handle (the sets of dots around the chart frame), and when the hollow double-headed arrow appears, drag in the direction you want the chart to grow or shrink.

To select a chart element

➜ Click the element once.

➜ If the element is difficult to identify or click, on the **Format** tool tab, in the **Current Selection** group, display the **Chart Elements** list, and then click the element you want.

Tip If you want to activate the chart (that is, select the chart area), be sure to click a blank area inside the chart frame. Clicking any of the chart's elements will activate that element, not the chart as a whole.

To change the size of a selected chart element

→ Point to any handle, and when the hollow double-headed arrow appears, drag in the direction you want the element to grow or shrink.

Tip If an element cannot be sized, the hollow double-headed arrow does not appear.

To change the position of a selected chart element

→ Point to the border around the element, away from any handles, and when the four-headed arrow appears, drag to the desired position.

Tip Some elements cannot be moved, even if the four-headed arrow appears.

To rotate a three-dimensional chart layout

1. Right-click the chart, and then click **3-D Rotation**.
2. In the **3-D Rotation** area of the **Effects** page of the **Format Chart Area** pane, set the angle of rotation for each axis.

Format charts

You can modify and format a chart to get the effect you want. If you don't want to spend a lot of time on individual chart elements, you can apply styles (predefined combinations of formatting) to the chart area (the entire chart) to create sophisticated charts with a minimum of effort.

Quick Styles include the following:

- **Chart styles** Combinations of data marker, wall, and floor fill colors, background color, and bevel effects
- **Shape styles** Combinations of shape fills, shape outlines, and shape effects
- **WordArt styles** Combinations of text fills, text outlines, and text effects

You can also apply shape style and WordArt style components individually, both to the chart area and to a selected chart element.

In addition to using styles and style components, you can fine-tune the formatting of a selected chart element in its Format pane. Each type of element has a specific Format pane. Most Format panes have multiple pages presenting options such as:

- **Chart area** You can specify the background fill, the border color and style, effects such as shadows and edges, the 3-D format and rotation, and the size and position. You can also attach text to be displayed when someone points to the chart.
- **Plot area** You can specify the background fill, the border color and style, effects such as shadows and edges, and the 3-D format and rotation.

- **Data markers** You can specify the background fill, the border color and style, effects such as shadows and edges, and the 3-D format. You can also precisely determine the gap between data points.

- **Legend** You can specify the background fill, the border color and style, and effects such as shadows and edges. You can also specify the legend's position and whether it can overlap the chart.

- **Axes** You can specify the background fill, the line color and style, effects such as shadows and edges, and the 3-D format and rotation. For the category axis, you can also specify the scale, add or remove tick marks, adjust the label position, and determine the starting and maximum values. You can set the number format (such as currency or percentage), and set the axis label alignment.

- **Gridlines** You can set the line color, line style, and effects such as shadows and edges.

- **Data table** You can specify the background fill, the border color and style, effects such as shadows and edges, and the 3-D format. You can also set table borders.

- **Titles** You can specify the background fill, the border color and style, effects such as shadows and edges, and the 3-D format. You can also set the title's alignment, direction, and angle of rotation.

To apply a chart style to a selected chart

➜ On the **Design** tool tab, in the **Chart Styles** gallery, click the style you want.

To apply a shape style to a selected chart component

➜ On the **Format** tool tab, in the **Shape Styles** gallery, click the style you want.

To apply shape style components to a selected chart component

➜ In the **Shape Styles** group, click the **Shape Fill**, **Shape Outline**, or **Shape Effects** button, and then click the option you want.

To apply a WordArt style to the text in a selected chart

➜ On the **Format** tool tab, in the **WordArt Styles** gallery, click the style you want.

To apply WordArt style components to a selected chart component

➜ In the **WordArt Styles** group, click the **Text Fill**, **Text Outline**, or **Text Effects** button, and then click the option you want.

To display the Format pane for a chart element

→ If the element is easy to identify, simply double-click it.

→ Right-click the element, and then click **Format** *Element*.

→ At the top of an open **Format** pane, click the downward-pointing triangle to the right of the **Options** label, and then click the element for which you want to display the Format pane.

Format Data Labels ▼ ✕
Label Options ▼   Text Options

◢ **Label Options**
  Label Contains
    ☐ Value From Cells
    ☐ Series Name
    ☐ Category Name
    ☑ Value
    ☑ Show Leader Lines
    ☐ Legend key
  Separator   [,   ▼]
    [Reset Label Text]
  Label Position
    ○ Center
    ◉ Inside End
    ○ Inside Base
    ○ Outside End
▷ **Number**

Chart Area
Horizontal (Category) Axis
Horizontal (Category) Axis Title
Legend
Plot Area
Vertical (Value) Axis
Vertical (Value) Axis Major Gridlines
Vertical (Value) Axis Minor Gridlines
Vertical (Value) Axis Title
Series "North"
Series "North" Data Labels
Series "West"
Series "West" Data Labels
Series "East"
Series "East" Data Labels
Series "South"
Series "South" Data Labels

Clicking the Label Options arrow displays a menu of labels you can format

Or

1. If you have trouble double-clicking a smaller chart element, on the **Format** tool tab, in the **Current Selection** group, display the **Chart Elements** list, and then click the element you want.

2. In the **Current Selection** group, click the **Format Selection** button.

Tip To display the Format Major Gridlines pane, right-click any gridline, and then click Format Gridlines. To display the Format Data Table pane, right-click the selected data table, and then click Format Data Table.

Objective 3.2 practice tasks

The practice file for these tasks is located in the **MOSPowerPoint2016 \Objective3** practice file folder. The folder also contains a result file that you can use to check your work.

➤ Open the **PowerPoint_3-2a** presentation, display slide 1, and do the following:

- ☐ Use the data from cells A3:C9 of the worksheet in the **PowerPoint_3-2b** workbook to create a Clustered Column chart.
- ☐ Change the Average data point for Brushing Teeth to <u>4</u> and the Conservative data point to <u>2</u>.
- ☐ Change the chart type to *Stacked Line With Markers*.
- ☐ Apply *Quick Layout 3*.
- ☐ Set the chart title to <u>Water Consumption (Gallons)</u>.

➤ Display slide 2 and do the following:

- ☐ Switch the rows and columns so that the columns are clustered by month and the legend identifies the Minimum, Average, and Maximum series.

➤ Display slide 3 and do the following:

- ☐ Apply *Style 7* to the entire chart.
- ☐ Select the chart area, and apply the *Intense Effect – Orange, Accent 6* shape style.
- ☐ Select the chart title, and apply the *Fill: White; Outline: Green, Accent color 1; Glow: Green, Accent color 1* WordArt Quick Style.
- ☐ For each pie slice, explode the data points in the chart by 20 percent. Then set the angle of the first slice at 200.
- ☐ Change the chart legend position from Bottom to Right.

➤ Save the **PowerPoint_3-2a** presentation.

➤ Open the **PowerPoint_3-2_results** presentation. Compare the two presentations to check your work.

➤ Close the open presentations.

Objective 3.3:
Insert and format SmartArt graphics

When you want to clearly illustrate a concept such as a process, cycle, hierarchy, or relationship, the powerful SmartArt Graphics tool makes it easy to create dynamic, visually appealing diagrams.

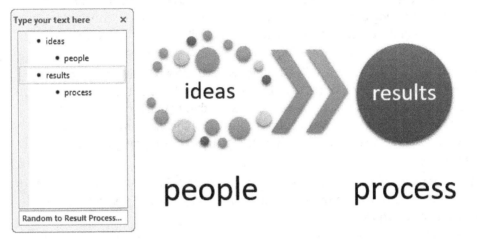

SmartArt text is stored as a bulleted list

The content of the diagram is controlled by a single-level or multiple-level list. The appearance is controlled by the SmartArt template. By using the available templates, you can easily construct any of the following types of diagrams:

- **List** These diagrams visually represent lists of related or independent information—for example, a list of items needed to complete a task, including pictures of the items.

- **Process** These diagrams visually describe the ordered set of steps required to complete a task—for example, the steps for getting a project approved.

- **Cycle** These diagrams represent a circular sequence of steps, tasks, or events, or the relationship of a set of steps, tasks, or events to a central, core element—for example, the looping process for continually improving a product based on customer feedback.

- **Hierarchy** These diagrams illustrate the structure of an organization or entity—for example, the top-level management structure of a company.

- **Relationship** These diagrams show convergent, divergent, overlapping, merging, or containment elements—for example, how using similar methods to organize your email, calendar, and contacts can improve your productivity.

- **Matrix** These diagrams show the relationship of components to a whole—for example, the product teams in a department.
- **Pyramid** These diagrams illustrate proportional or interconnected relationships—for example, the amount of time that should ideally be spent on different phases of a project.
- **Picture** These diagrams rely on pictures in addition to text to create one of the other types of diagrams—for example, a process picture diagram with photographs showing changes in a natural formation over time. Picture diagrams are a subset of the other categories but are also available from their own category so that you can easily locate diagram layouts that support images.

In PowerPoint (but not in other Office programs), you can easily convert an ordinary bulleted list to a SmartArt graphic that retains the relationship of the bullet levels. Or you can create the diagram and then add text, either directly to its shapes or as a bulleted list in the Text pane, which opens to the left of the diagram. In the Text pane, you can add shapes, delete shapes, and rearrange them by dragging the associated list items.

SmartArt graphic layouts are available from the Choose A SmartArt Graphic dialog box. The categories are not mutually exclusive, meaning that some layouts appear in more than one category.

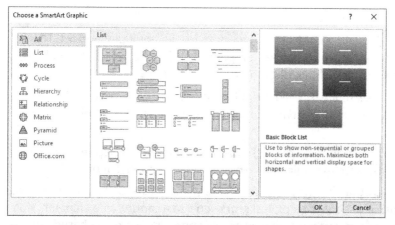

Choose a category based on the type of information you want to present

After you choose a layout, PowerPoint inserts the basic diagram into the slide and displays the associated list format in the Text pane, into which you can enter information. (If the Text pane doesn't open automatically, you can display it by clicking the button on the left edge of the diagram.) You can enter more or less information than is depicted by the original diagram; most diagrams support a range of entries (although a few are formatted to support only a specific number of entries). You can insert and modify text either directly in the diagram shapes or in the associated Text pane. The SmartArt layout determines whether the text appears in or adjacent to its shapes.

> **Tip** You change the size, shape, and location of a SmartArt graphic by using the same techniques you use with other graphic elements.

After you create a diagram and add the text you want to display in it, you might find that the diagram layout you originally selected doesn't precisely meet your needs. You can easily change to a different diagram layout without losing any of the information you entered in the diagram. If a particular layout doesn't support the amount or level of information that is associated with the diagram, the extra text will be hidden but not deleted, and will be available when you choose another layout that supports it.

> **Tip** If a gallery has a sizing handle (three dots) in its lower-right corner, you can resize it. By reducing the height of the gallery, you can display more of the slide and the gallery at the same time.

When you decide on the layout you want to use, you can add and remove shapes and edit the text of the diagram either by making changes in the Text pane or by using the options on the SmartArt tool tabs.

You can make changes such as the following by using the commands on the Design tool tab:

- Add shading and three-dimensional effects to all the shapes in a diagram.
- Change the color scheme.

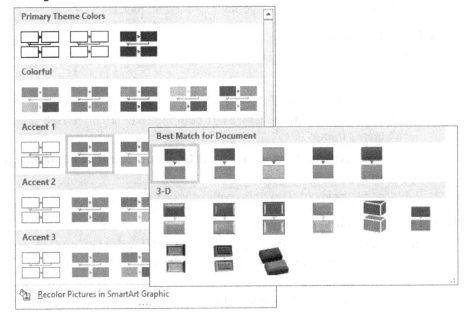

The available colors are based on the presentation theme color scheme

- Add shapes and change their hierarchy.
- Reverse the order of shapes.

You can customize individual shapes in the following ways:

- Change an individual shape—for example, change a square into a star.
- Apply a built-in shape style.
- Change the color, outline, or effect of a shape.
- Change the style of the shape's text.

The Live Preview feature displays the effects of these changes before you apply them. If you apply changes and then decide you preferred the original version, you can easily click the return to the unaltered diagram layout.

To create a SmartArt graphic from a bulleted list

→ Right-click any item in the list, click **Convert to SmartArt**, and then click the layout you want.

→ Right-click any item in the list, click **More SmartArt Graphics**, click a layout in the **Choose SmartArt Graphic** dialog box, and then click **OK**.

To create an empty SmartArt graphic

1. On the **Insert** tab, in the **Illustrations** group, click the **SmartArt** button.
2. In the left pane of the **Choose a SmartArt Graphic** dialog box, click the type of diagram you want.
3. In the center pane, click the layout you want, and then click **OK**.

To add text to a SmartArt graphic

→ Click a shape, and then enter the text.

Or

1. Open the **Text** pane by doing one of the following:
   - Click the button (labeled with a left-pointing chevron) on the left side of the diagram's frame.
   - On the **Design** tool tab, in the **Create Graphic** group, click the **Text Pane** button.
2. Replace the placeholder list items with your own text.

To add a shape to a SmartArt graphic

→ In the **Text** pane, at the right end of the bullet after which you want to add the shape, press **Enter**, and then enter the text for the new shape.

→ Click the shape before or after which you want to add the new shape. On the **Design** tool tab, in the **Create Graphic** group, do either of the following:
   - To add a shape after the selected shape, click the **Add Shape** button.
   - To add a shape before the selected shape, click the **Add Shape** arrow and then click **Add Shape Before**.

To promote or demote a first-level diagram shape to a subordinate entry

→ On the **Design** tool tab, in the **Create Graphic** group, click the **Promote** or **Demote** button.

→ In the **Text** pane, click at the left end of an entry, and then press **Tab** to demote it or **Shift+Tab** to promote it.

Tip Some SmartArt diagrams are not formatted to accept subordinate entries.

To move an existing shape

→ Drag the shape to the new location.

→ On the **Design** tool tab, in the **Create Graphic** group, click the **Move Up** or **Move Down** button.

To reverse the order of shapes in a SmartArt graphic

→ On the **Design** tool tab, in the **Create Graphic** group, click the **Right To Left** button.

To delete a shape from a SmartArt graphic

→ In the diagram, click the shape, and then press the **Delete** key.

→ In the **Text** pane, select the list item, and then press the **Delete** key.

To change the color scheme of a selected diagram

→ On the **Design** tool tab, in the **SmartArt Styles** group, click the **Change Colors** button, and then click the color scheme you want.

To apply a style to a selected diagram

→ On the **Design** tool tab, in the **SmartArt Styles** gallery, click the style you want to apply.

To apply a style to a selected diagram shape

→ On the **Format** tool tab, in the **Shape Styles** gallery, click the style you want to apply.

Or

1. On the **Format** tool tab, click the **Shape Styles** dialog box launcher.

2. In the **Format Shape** pane, on the **Fill & Line**, **Effects**, and **Layout & Properties** pages, choose the effects that you want to apply.

To reset diagram modifications

→ On the **Design** tool tab, in the **Reset** group, click the **Reset Graphic** button.

> **Exam Strategy** Many formatting options are available from the Design and Format tool tabs. Be familiar with the options available on the tool tabs and in the associated dialog boxes.

Objective 3.3 practice tasks

The practice file for these tasks is located in the **MOSPowerPoint2016 \Objective3** practice file folder. The folder also contains a result file that you can use to check your work.

➤ Open the **PowerPoint_3-3** presentation, display slide 3, and do the following:

- ❑ Insert a *Half Circle Organization Chart* SmartArt graphic.
- ❑ In the manager's position at the top of the organization chart, enter your name.
- ❑ Enter <u>Joan</u> as your assistant.
- ❑ Enter <u>Jaime</u>, <u>Kathy</u>, and <u>Susie</u> as the three employees.
- ❑ Delete your assistant from the organization chart, and then add <u>Joan</u> as an assistant to Susie.
- ❑ Change the color scheme of the organization chart to *Colored Outline – Accent 1* (in the *Accent 1* section).

➤ Display slide 4 and do the following:

- ❑ Convert the bulleted list to a *Continuous Block Process* SmartArt graphic.
- ❑ Change the layout to *Basic Venn* (in the *Relationship* category).
- ❑ Change the style to *Polished* (in the *3-D* section).
- ❑ Change the colors to *Colorful – Accent Colors* (in the *Colorful* section).
- ❑ Apply the *Fill: Black, Text color 1; Shadow* WordArt style to the diagram text.
- ❑ Select the *Administration & Human Resources* shape and change its fill color to *Dark Red* (in the *Standard Colors* palette).

➤ Save the **PowerPoint_3-3** presentation.

➤ Open the **PowerPoint_3-3_results** presentation. Compare the two presentations to check your work.

➤ Close the open presentations.

Objective 3.4: Insert and manage media

Embed audio and video clips

There are many ways of communicating information to audiences. PowerPoint is primarily a visual medium through which a presenter displays static information. However, PowerPoint presentations can also include sound and video.

In addition to the sound effects that are available for slide transitions, you can play audio clips for a specific length of time or throughout an entire slide show. For example, you might include light background music during a slide show that plays repeatedly while an audience is entering the room, emphasize a point by playing a sound clip, or prerecord the audio presentation for each slide. You can insert audio clips from a local source or record them directly in PowerPoint.

If part of the information that you want to convey to your audience is in video form, you can embed that video on a slide instead of having to play it from a different device. This helps to keep your audience focused on your presentation, and simplifies the setup necessary to present the video. You can insert video clips from an online or local source.

3

You can generate embed codes from online video services

When you insert an audio clip on a slide, a translucent speaker icon appears in the center of the slide. You can move or resize the icon, and hide it during a slide show. When the speaker icon is selected, PowerPoint displays a Play/Pause button, a progress bar, an elapsed time counter, and a volume control.

To embed an existing audio clip on a slide

1. Save the audio clip on your computer, a connected drive, or a network-connected location.

2. On the **Insert** tab, in the **Media** group, click the **Audio** button, and then click **Audio on My PC**.

3. In the **Insert Audio** dialog box, browse to the audio file location, click the audio file or thumbnail, and then click **Insert**.

To record and embed an audio clip

1. On the **Insert** tab, in the **Media** group, click the **Audio** button, and then click **Record Audio**.

2. In the **Record Sound** dialog box, enter a name for the audio clip, and then click the **Record** button (the red dot).

3. Deliver the audio content that you want to record, and when you finish, click the **Stop** button (the blue square).

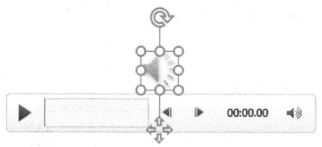

You can rename the clip before or after recording it

4. Do any of the following:

   - Click the **Play** button to play back the audio clip.
   - Click the **Record** button to re-record the audio clip.
   - Click **Cancel** to close the dialog box without saving the audio clip.
   - Click **OK** to embed the recorded audio on the slide.

When not selected, the audio icon can be difficult to see against a busy slide background

To insert a local video clip

1. Do either of the following:

    - In a content placeholder, click the **Insert Video** button. Then in the **Insert Video** window, click **From a file**.

    - On the **Insert** tab, in the **Media** group, click the **Video** button, and then click **Video on My PC**.

2. In the **Insert Video** window, browse to the video location, click the video file or thumbnail, and click **Insert**.

To insert an online video clip

➜ Do either of the following:

    - In a content placeholder, click the **Insert Video** button.

    - On the **Insert** tab, in the **Media** group, click the **Video** button, and then click **Online Video**.

    - In the **Insert Video** window, click the video source. Then browse to the video location, click the video file or thumbnail, and click **Insert**.

Modify audio and video clips

You can configure audio to play automatically, to play for a specific amount of time, or to loop continuously during a specific slide or the entire presentation. You can fade gradually into and out of an audio clip. You can also trim the audio clip to play only a specific portion of it.

Specify the points in an audio or video clip that you want to start and finish playback

After you insert a video clip, you can resize the window it appears in, or even crop the area of the video that is displayed. By default, a video clip plays within its window, but you can configure it to play at full-screen size. You can also configure most of the same playback options for video clips that you can for audio clips, and you can apply the standard picture styles to the video window.

It isn't necessary to edit audio or video prior to inserting it in a presentation. You can trim audio and video clips in much the same way that you can format the appearance of a picture: although the audience hears or sees only what you select, the original media is unaltered.

To modify the appearance of a selected audio icon or video window

→ On the **Format** tool tab, in the **Adjust**, **Picture Styles**, or **Video Styles** group, configure the formatting options you want.

To trim an audio or video clip

1. On the **Playback** tool tab, click the **Trim Audio** or **Trim Video** button.
2. In the **Trim Audio** or **Trim Video** dialog box, drag the **Start** and **End** sliders, or set the **Start Time** and **End Time**.
3. Preview the results and make adjustments as necessary, and then click **OK** to apply the trim.

To transition into or out of an audio or video clip

→ On the **Playback** tool tab, in the **Editing** group, set the **Fade In** and **Fade Out** times.

To configure the playback options for an audio clip

→ On the **Playback** tool tab, in the **Audio Options** group, do any of the following:

- Click **Volume**, and then click **Low**, **Medium**, **High**, or **Mute**.
- In the **Start** list, click **On Click** or **Automatically**.
- Select the **Play Across Slides** check box to continue playing the clip when the next slide is displayed.
- Select the **Loop until Stopped** check box to automatically restart the clip when it ends.
- Select the **Hide During Show** check box to hide the audio icon when the slide is shown.
- Select the **Rewind after Playing** check box to automatically return to the beginning of the clip when it finishes.

→ On the **Playback** tool tab, in the **Audio Styles** group, click the **Play in Background** button to set the audio options necessary to play the clip continuously from the slide on which it starts until the presentation ends or the clip is stopped.

To configure the playback options for a video clip

→ On the **Playback** tool tab, in the **Video Options** group, do any of the following:

- Click **Volume**, and then click **Low**, **Medium**, **High**, or **Mute**.
- In the **Start** list, click **On Click** or **Automatically**.
- Select the **Play Full Screen** check box to expand the video to full-screen size while it is playing.
- Select the **Hide While Not Playing** check box to hide the video window after the video ends.
- Select the **Loop until Stopped** check box to automatically restart the clip when it ends.
- Select the **Rewind after Playing** check box to automatically return to the beginning of the clip when it finishes.

To resize a video window

→ Drag the window sizing handles.

→ On the **Format** tool tab, in the **Size** group, set the **Video Height** or **Video Width**, and then press **Enter**.

→ On the **Format** tool tab, click the **Size** dialog box launcher. In the **Format Video** pane, configure the height, width, rotation, scale, and aspect ratio settings.

To crop a video window

1. On the **Format** tool tab, in the **Size** group, click the **Crop** button.
2. Drag the crop handles to frame the portion of the video window that you want to display.

Tip Drag the crop frame to move it to a different part of the video window.

---

3. Click the **Crop** button again to apply the changes.

3

Objective 3.4 practice tasks

The practice file for these tasks is located in the **MOSPowerPoint2016 \Objective3** practice file folder. The folder also contains a result file that you can use to check your work.

➤ Open the **PowerPoint_3-4a** presentation and do the following:

- ❏ On slide 1, insert the **PowerPoint_3-4b** audio clip from the practice file folder. The audio clip is 2 minutes in length.
- ❏ Configure the audio playback options to play the audio clip as a soundtrack to the presentation.
- ❏ On slide 2, insert the **PowerPoint_3-4c** video clip from the practice file folder. The video clip is 2 minutes, 40 seconds in length.
- ❏ Trim the video to 1 minute, starting 25 seconds into the original clip.
- ❏ Configure the video to start automatically when the slide appears, and to fade out over the last 5 seconds of the video.
- ❏ Mute the sound of the video so that it does not compete with the audio soundtrack.
- ❏ Set the video frame style to *Rotated, White* (in the *Moderate* section).
- ❏ Resize the video frame to <u>6.0"</u> wide and maintain the original aspect ratio.
- ❏ Center the video frame horizontally and align it with the bottom of the slide title.
- ❏ Test the soundtrack and video by playing the slide show.

➤ Save the **PowerPoint_3-4a** presentation.

➤ Open the **PowerPoint_3-4_results** presentation. Compare the two presentations to check your work.

➤ Close the open presentations.

Objective group 4

Apply transitions and animations

The skills tested in this section of the Microsoft Office Specialist exam for Microsoft PowerPoint 2016 relate to applying slide transitions, animating slide content, and setting timing for transitions and animations. Specifically, the following objectives are associated with this set of skills:

4.1 Apply slide transitions

4.2 Animate slide content

4.3 Set timing for transitions and animations

When you deliver a presentation, you can move from slide to slide by clicking the mouse button, or you can have PowerPoint replace one slide with the next at predetermined intervals. One of the ways in which you can keep an audience's attention is by applying an interesting transition effect when moving between slides. Another way to keep the audience's interest, and often to communicate additional information, is to animate text and objects on slides. By incorporating dynamic effects, you can emphasize key points, control the focus of the discussion, and entertain in ways that will make your message memorable.

This chapter guides you in studying ways of configuring slide transitions and animating slide content.

4

> To complete the practice tasks in this chapter, you need the practice files contained in the **MOSPowerPoint2016\Objective4** practice file folder. For more information, see "Download the practice files" in this book's introduction.

Objective 4.1: Apply slide transitions

Transitions control the way slides move into and out of view during a slide show. They include simple effects such as sliding in, more complex effects such as dissolving in from the outer edges or the center, and very fancy effects such as scattering the slide content like glitter. All the base transition effects are available in the Transitions gallery.

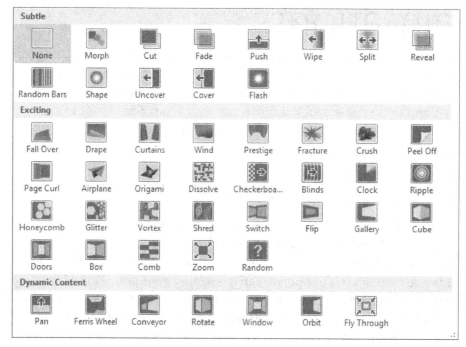

Transition effects are divided into three categories: Subtle, Exciting, and Dynamic Content

The transition from one slide to the next is controlled by the transition applied to the incoming slide. Each slide can have only one transition effect. You can set transitions in Normal view or Slide Sorter view. You can set a transition for one slide, for a group of slides, or for an entire presentation.

Depending on the type of transition, you might be able to further refine its effect by clicking a specific option on the related Effect Options menu. In addition to any available effect options, you can specify the following:

- An associated sound
- The transition speed
- When the transition occurs

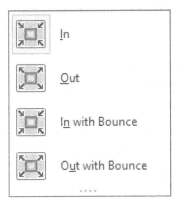

The available effect options are specific to the currently applied effect

As with all effects, be careful not to overdo it. Consider the tone and purpose of a presentation when applying transitions.

See Also For information about transition speed and triggers, see "Objective 4.3: Set timing for transitions and animations."

To apply a transition to a selected slide or slides

➜ On the **Transitions** tab, in the **Transition to This Slide** group, display the **Transitions** gallery, and then click the transition you want.

To modify transition effect options

➜ In the **Transition to This Slide** group, click the **Effect Options** button, and then click the effect you want.

To incorporate a sound into the transition of a selected slide

➜ On the **Transitions** tab, in the **Timing** group, display the **Sound** list, and then click the sound you want.

➜ In the **Timing** group, in the **Sound** list, click **Other Sound**. In the **Add Audio** dialog box, locate and select the sound file you want to use, and then click **Open**.

To apply the transition of the selected slide to all the slides

➜ In the **Timing** group, click the **Apply To All** button.

To remove transitions between slides

1. On the **Transitions** tab, in the **Transition to This Slide** group, display the **Transitions** gallery, and click **None**.

2. In the **Timing** group, click the **Apply To All** button.

4

Objective 4.1 practice tasks

The practice file for these tasks is located in the **MOSPowerPoint2016 \Objective4** practice file folder. The folder also contains a result file that you can use to check your work.

➤ Open the **PowerPoint_4-1** presentation and do the following:
- ☐ Apply the *Cover* transition to all the slides in the presentation.
- ☐ Make the transition effect begin from the bottom.
- ☐ Add the *Wind* sound to the transition.
- ☐ Set the transition duration to <u>3</u> seconds.
- ☐ Remove the slide transition effect from only slide 1.

➤ Save the **PowerPoint_4-1** presentation.

➤ Open the **PowerPoint_4-1_results** presentation. Compare the two presentations to check your work.

➤ Close the open presentations.

Objective 4.2: Animate slide content

If you are delivering a presentation from your computer, you can keep your audience focused and reinforce your message by animating slide elements such as text and graphics.

Apply animations

Many common animations are available from the Animation gallery. These animations fall into four categories depending on their purpose:

- **Entrance** Animate the appearance (arrival) of an element on the slide.
- **Emphasis** Draw attention to an element by changing its size or appearance, or by making it move.
- **Exit** Animate the departure of an element from the slide.
- **Motion Paths** Move an element from one location on the slide to another, along a specific path.

You can access additional animations in each category by clicking the *More* commands at the bottom of the Animation menu. Entrance, Emphasis, and Exit effects are classified in subcategories of Basic, Subtle, Moderate, and Exciting to help you match the effects with the tone of your presentation.

The available effects depend on the currently selected object

Path effects are classified in subcategories of Basic, Lines & Curves, and Special to reflect the type and direction of movement in the motion path.

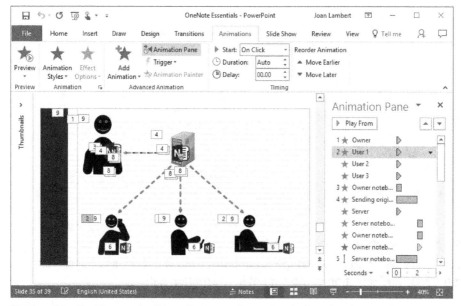

You can build on more than 60 motion paths to precisely animate slide content

You can apply multiple animation effects to an object. On the slide and in the Animation pane, each animation is identified by an adjacent numbered box that indicates the order in which the animations will occur.

Numbers identify objects on the slide and corresponding actions in the Animation pane

To apply an animation from the gallery to a selected object

➜ On the **Animations** tab, in the **Advanced Animation** group, click **Add Animation**, and then click the animation you want.

Each entrance effect has a corresponding exit effect

To apply an animation that doesn't appear in the gallery

1. On the **Animations** tab, in the **Advanced Animation** group, click the **Add Animation** button, and then at the bottom of the gallery, click the animation category you want.

2. In the **Add** *Animation* **Effect** dialog box, click the animation you want.

To change the animation applied to a selected object

➜ On the **Animations** tab, in the **Animation** group, click **Animation Styles**, and then click the animation you want to use.

To remove an animation from a selected object

➜ In the **Animation** gallery, click **None**.

To apply additional animation to a selected animated object

➔ On the **Animations** tab, in the **Advanced Animation** group, click the **Add Animation** button, and then click the animation you want to add.

To copy the animations applied to a selected object to another object

➔ In the **Advanced Animation** group, click the **Animation Painter** button, and then click the object to which you want to copy the animations.

To display the Animation pane

➔ On the **Animations** tab, in the **Advanced Animation** group, click the **Animation Pane** button.

To preview animations

➔ To preview the animation of the selected object, on the **Animations** tab, in the **Preview** group, click the **Preview** button.

➔ To preview all animations on the slide, click a blank area of the slide and then in the **Animation** pane, click **Play All**.

➔ To preview some animations, in the **Animation** pane, click the animation you want to start with, and then click **Play From**.

Configure animation effects

The animation names reflect the basic action of each animation. After you apply an animation effect, you can fine-tune its action by using the commands on the Animations tab. Depending on the basic action of the animation and the element you are animating, you can configure one or more of the following settings for an animation: Amount, Color, Direction, Number of spokes, Sequence, Shape, and Vanishing point.

The available effect options vary based on the specific animation. Many animations, such as Appear/Disappear, Fade, Grow & Turn/Shrink & Turn, Swivel, Bounce, Pulse, Teeter, Desaturate, Darken, and Lighten don't have effect options when applied to individual objects, but you can customize other aspects of the animation such as the associated sound, the action of the object after the animation finishes, and the timing aspects such as trigger, duration, and delay.

You can manage animations by using tools on the ribbon and in the Animation pane, which displays a visual description of the animation sequence occurring on a slide.

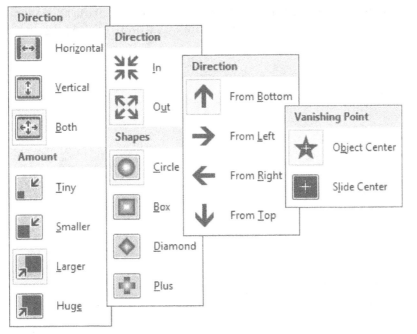

The effect option thumbnails provide visual guidance for making selections

Several information points are visible for each animation:

- The number (corresponding to the number next to the animated object on the slide) indicates the order in which a manually triggered animation occurs. An unnumbered animation starts in relation to the numbered animation it follows.

- The icon indicates the animation category. A green star indicates an entrance effect, a yellow star indicates an emphasis effect, a red star indicates an exit effect, and a blue double-ended line indicates a motion path. The specific animation is not indicated by the icon.

- The description indicates the object being animated.

> **Tip** Object names can be edited in the Selection pane. For information about the Selection pane, see "Objective 2.4: Order and group objects."

- The Advanced Timeline displays a triangle or bar that indicates the duration of the animation. The color of the triangle or bar corresponds to the animation category (green, yellow, red, or blue).

> **Tip** The display of the Advanced Timeline can be controlled from the Animation pane object shortcut menu.

- The timing bar at the bottom of the Animation pane indicates the time scale. The time scale can be modified by clicking the time unit to the left of the timing bar (Seconds, by default) and then clicking Zoom In or Zoom Out.

Pointing to an animation in the Animation pane displays a summary of the animation information in a ScreenTip. Clicking an animation displays an arrow. Clicking the arrow displays a list of actions.

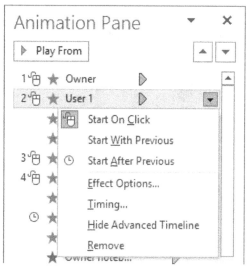

Control the settings for individual animations

Clicking Effect Options in the list displays a dialog box of options specific to the effect.

Refine options for an animation effect

Depending on the type of animation, the refinements you might be able to make include the following:

- Change the animation direction.
- Specify whether the animation should be accompanied by a sound.
- Dim or hide the object after the animation, or make it change to a specific color.
- If the animation is applied to text, animate all the text at once, word by word, or letter by letter.
- Change the Start, Delay, and Duration settings, repeat the animation, and specify what will trigger its action.
- If a slide has more than one level of bullet points, animate different levels separately.
- If an object has embedded text, animate the object and the text together (the default) or separately, or animate one but not the other.
- Specify whether a sequenced animation progresses forward or backward.

To select an animation for further configuration

→ On the slide, click the animation number.

→ In the **Animation** pane, click the animation number or description.

To configure basic effect options for a selected animation

→ In the **Animation** group, click the **Effect Options** button.

→ On the **Effect Options** menu (or in each section of the menu, if it has multiple sections), click the option you want.

To open the *Animation Style* dialog box of options for an animation

→ On the **Animations** tab, click the **Animation** dialog box launcher.

Or

1. In the **Animation** pane, do either of the following:
   - Click the animation and then click the arrow that appears.
   - Right-click the animation.
2. On the menu, click **Effect Options**.

To configure advanced effect options for a selected animation

1. Select the animated object, and open the *Animation Style* dialog box of options.
2. On the **Effect** tab, do any of the following:
   - To add sound to an animation, in the **Sound** list, click the sound you want.
   - To dim, hide, or change the color of text or an object after its animation completes, in the **After animation** list, click the color or effect you want.

4

- To animate all the text in a container at once, in the **Animate text** list, click **All at once**.
- To animate the text in a container by word, in the **Animate text** list, click **By word**.
- To animate the text in a container by letter, in the **Animate text** list, click **By letter**.

3. Click **OK** to close the dialog box and implement the changes.

To change the way multiple paragraphs of text are animated

→ On the **Animations** tab, in the **Animation** group, click **Effect Options** and then click **As One Object**, **All At Once**, or **By Paragraph**.

→ Open the **Effect Options** dialog box. On the **Text Animation** tab, expand the **Group text** list and then click **As One Object**, **All Paragraphs At Once**, or the paragraph level by which you want to group the text.

To change the order in which text is animated

→ Open the **Effect Options** dialog box. On the **Text Animation** tab, select the **In reverse order** check box.

Configure motion paths

After you apply a Motion Path animation, you can modify the path that the animation follows. Regardless of whether the motion path is straight, shaped, or curved, it has a start point (a green triangle), a rotation handle, and sizing handles. If a motion path is straight or curved, and doesn't return to its start point, it also has an end point (a red triangle). You can adjust the path by using any of these tools.

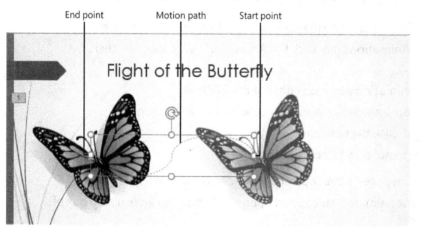

Selecting the animation path displays the object in its starting and ending positions

Moving any part of the animation path displays the animated object in both the starting and ending positions so you can gauge the effect of the move. When smart guides are turned on, you can use them to align the animated object with other slide elements.

It is important to note that you can move the animated object independent of its motion path so that the object moves from its original location on the slide to the beginning of the motion path, before following the motion path.

To adjust the height or length of the motion path of a selected animation

→ Drag the top, bottom, side, or corner handles.

To change the shape of the motion path of a selected animation

→ On the **Animations** tab, in the **Animation** group, click **Animation Styles**.

→ On the **Animation Styles** menu, do either of the following:

- In the **Motion Paths** section, click the shape you want.
- Click **More Motion Paths**. In the **Change Motion Path** dialog box, click the shape you want, and then click **OK**.

To rotate the motion path of a selected animation

→ Drag the rotation handle in a circular motion.

To change the angles of the motion path of a selected animation

1. On the **Animations** tab, in the **Animation** group, click **Effect Options**.
2. On the **Effect Options** menu, in the **Path** section, click **Edit Points**.
3. Drag any angle-change point to modify the path.

Each change in angle is represented by a movable point

To begin a motion path in a location other than the object location

→ Drag the object away from the start point of the motion path.

→ Drag the start point of the motion path away from the object.

To configure a custom motion path

→ Drag the object on the path you want it to follow. When you reach the end of the path, press the **Escape** key.

Objective 4.2 practice tasks

The practice file for these tasks is located in the **MOSPowerPoint2016
\Objective4** practice file folder. The folder also contains a result file that
you can use to check your work.

➤ Open the **PowerPoint_4-2** presentation, display slide 1 and do the
following:

❑ Select the slide title and apply the *Fly In* entrance animation.

❑ Configure the Fly In effect options to enter from the left side of the
slide.

❑ Set the animation duration to 1.00 second.

❑ Enhance the effect by applying the *Whoosh* sound effect.

➤ Display slide 2 and do the following:

❑ Select the slide title and apply the *Fade* entrance animation.

❑ Select the bulleted list and apply the *Pulse* emphasis animation.

❑ Configure the Pulse effect options to emphasize each bulleted list
item individually and to change the color of the list item to *Green*
after animating it.

❑ Use the Animation Painter to copy the animations from slide 2 to
the corresponding elements on slide 3.

➤ Display slide 4 and apply the following animations in order:

❑ Apply the *Teeter* emphasis animation to the butterfly.

❑ Apply the *Spin* emphasis animation to the bumblebee.

❑ Configure a *Custom Path* motion path animation that causes the
ladybug to walk on a curved path from its starting position to the
center of the content area.

❑ Apply the *Shrink & Turn* exit animation to the mouse.

❑ Apply the *Swivel* exit animation to the frog.

➤ Display the presentation in Slide Show view to review the results.

➤ Save the **PowerPoint_4-2** presentation.

➤ Open the **PowerPoint_4-2_results** presentation. Compare the two
presentations to check your work. Then close the open presentations.

Objective 4.3:
Set timing for transitions and animations

When you are incorporating slide transitions and animations into a presentation, two of the options you have for each of these are triggers and timing.

The trigger is the event that causes a transition or animation to begin. The default trigger for a transition or animation is On Mouse Click, meaning that the effect occurs when the presenter gives the signal to advance. When a slide includes animations that are set to start On Mouse Click, the signal to advance the slide instead runs the animation.

The timing of transitions and animations contributes to the tone of a presentation, particularly when the presentation is running automatically. All timing options can be entered in seconds but are expressed in the format *hh:mm:ss*.

Set timing for transitions

The timing options for transitions are in the Timing group on the Transitions tab. The Advance Slide options govern the time at or after which PowerPoint moves to the next slide. There are two Advance Slide options: On Mouse Click and After (which you set to a specific length of time). One or both of these options can be selected. If you plan to deliver a presentation in person, it is customary to retain the On Mouse Click trigger, and to advance the slide manually. Selecting the After check box and specifying a length of time causes PowerPoint to automatically transition to the next slide after that time interval. Selecting both check boxes permits the presenter to manually advance the slide before the specified time has elapsed.

The length of time from the beginning to the end of a transition effect is its duration. A short duration results in the full slide content appearing quickly, and a long duration results in it appearing slowly. Factors to consider when setting the duration include the type of content on the slide and the selected transition. For example, you might want to assign a short duration to a slide transition for which the slide content is not visible until the transition completes. You might assign a long duration to a transition that causes the slide content to appear in legible segments while you discuss it. PowerPoint recognizes the wait time required for various transition effects to deliver legible slide content; for this reason, the default transition duration varies based on the transition.

4

To manually trigger the transition to the next slide

→ On the **Transitions** tab, in the **Timing** group, select the **On Mouse Click** check box.

To automate the transition of the selected slide

1. On the **Transitions** tab, in the **Timing** group, clear the **On Mouse Click** check box.

2. Select the **After** check box, and then enter a time in the **adjacent** box.

To change the speed of the transition of a selected slide

→ In the **Timing** group, enter the number of seconds you want the transition to continue in the **Duration** box.

See Also For more information about slide timings, see "Objective 1.7: Configure and present a slide show."

Set timing and order for animations

The timing options for animations are in the Timing group on the Animations tab. Three timing options can be configured for each animation: Start, Duration, and Delay. The timing options are also expressed visually in the Animation pane.

There are three Start options: On Click, With Previous, and With Next. On Click runs the animation when the presenter gives the signal to advance, or clicks a specific trigger object on the slide. With Previous starts the animation at the same time as the preceding animation (or in the case of the first animation, immediately after the slide appears). With Next runs the animation and starts the next animation or action when the presenter gives the signal. The most common use for this setting is to run the final animation on the slide and then immediately transition to the next slide.

As with transitions, the Duration is the length of time from the beginning to the end of an animation effect. The Delay is the length of time PowerPoint waits after the trigger signal to play the animation.

To manually trigger a selected animation

→ Open the **Effect Options** dialog box. On the **Timing** tab, in the **Start** list, click **On Click**, **With Previous**, or **With Next**.

→ On the **Animations** tab, in the **Timing** group, in the **Start** list, click **On Click**.

To trigger an animation by clicking a specific object

➜ In the **Advanced Animation** group, click **Trigger**, click **On Click of**, and then click the trigger object.

Or

1. Open the **Effect Options** dialog box.
2. On the **Timing** tab, click **Triggers**.
3. Click **Start effect on click of**, and then in the list, click the object you want to use as a trigger.

To automate the start of the selected animation

➜ In the **Timing** group, in the **Start** list, click **With Previous**.

➜ Open the **Effect Options** dialog box. On the **Timing** tab, in the **Start** list, click **With Previous**, or **With Next**.

To automate the action after the selected animation

➜ In the **Timing** group, in the **Start** list, click **After Previous**.

➜ Open the **Effect Options** dialog box. On the **Timing** tab, in the **Start** list, click **On Click, With Previous**, or **With Next**.

To change the duration of an animation

➜ In the **Timing** group, enter the number of seconds you want the animation to continue in the **Duration** box.

➜ Open the **Effect Options** dialog box. On the **Timing** tab, in the **Duration** list, click **5 seconds (Very Slow), 3 seconds (Slow), 2 seconds (Medium), 1 seconds (Fast)**, or **0.5 seconds (Very Fast)**.

To delay the start of an animation

➜ In the **Timing** group, enter the number of seconds you want to delay the animation in the **Delay** box.

➜ Open the **Effect Options** dialog box. On the **Timing** tab, in the **Delay** box, enter the delay in seconds.

To change the order of animations applied to a selected object

➜ On the **Animations** tab, in the **Reorder Animation** area of the **Timing** group, click **Move Earlier** or **Move Later**.

➜ In the upper-right corner of the **Animation** pane, click the **Move Earlier** or **Move Later** arrow.

4

Objective 4.3 practice tasks

The practice file for these tasks is located in the **MOSPowerPoint2016 \Objective4** practice file folder. The folder also contains a result file that you can use to check your work.

➤ Open the **PowerPoint_4-3** presentation, display slide 1, and do the following:

- ❑ Configure the title animation to start automatically when the slide appears.
- ❑ Configure the subtitle animation to start automatically, <u>2.00</u> seconds after the title animation.

➤ Display slide 2 and do the following:

- ❑ Configure the title animation to start automatically when the slide appears.
- ❑ Set the duration of the title animation to <u>1.50</u> seconds.
- ❑ Configure the bulleted list animations to start automatically, <u>2.00</u> seconds after the title animation.
- ❑ Set the duration of the bulleted list animations to <u>1.50</u> seconds.

➤ Display slide 3 and do the following:

- ❑ Configure the title animation to animate letter by letter, with a 50 percent delay between letter.

➤ Display slide 4 and do the following:

- ❑ Change the order of the animations to ladybug, mouse, bee, frog, and then butterfly.

➤ Save the **PowerPoint_4-3** presentation.

➤ Open the **PowerPoint_4-3_results** presentation. Compare the two presentations to check your work.

➤ Close the open presentations.

Objective group 5

Manage multiple presentations

The skills tested in this section of the Microsoft Office Specialist exam for Microsoft PowerPoint 2016 relate to merging content from multiple presentations and finalizing presentations. Specifically, the following objectives are associated with this set of skills:

5.1 Merge content from multiple presentations

5.2 Finalize presentations

When working with colleagues to develop a presentation, you might each develop a separate part of the presentation and then merge the presentations into one, or you might work in multiple versions of the whole presentation and then merge those into one. During the collaboration process, it is frequently necessary to review changes made by one or more people and decide which version of the content to retain.

When you and your colleagues need to communicate about a presentation that you're developing, one method of doing so is by inserting information in comments attached to specific slides or slide content.

This chapter guides you in studying ways of reusing content from one presentation in another, comparing and merging multiple versions of a presentation, using the commenting tools, inspecting presentations for issues, and preparing presentations for distribution.

5

To complete the practice tasks in this chapter, you need the practice files contained in the **MOSPowerPoint2016\Objective5** practice file folder. For more information, see "Download the practice files" in this book's introduction.

Objective 5.1:
Merge content from multiple presentations

Display multiple presentations

PowerPoint displays each presentation you open in its own program window. As a result, you can not only switch among open presentations, but you can also view multiple presentations simultaneously. You can display windows side by side or in a cascading arrangement so that you can easily click the one you want.

When you want to view two different parts of the same presentation, you can open a second instance of the presentation in a separate window, arrange the windows side by side, and then scroll the windows independently. (In fact, you can open many instances of a presentation.) Each window is identified in the title bar by the instance number after the file name. Changes that you make to any instance of the open presentation are immediately reflected in all instances.

To display more than one presentation at the same time

1. Open the presentations that you want to display.
2. On the **View** tab, in the **Window** group, do either of the following:
   - To arrange the open program windows side by side, click **Arrange All**.
   - To arrange the open program windows in an overlapping formation, click **Cascade**.

Tip You can use standard Windows window-management techniques to move PowerPoint program windows on the screen and snap them to the sides or quadrants of the screen.

To display the same presentation in multiple windows

1. On the **View** tab, in the **Window** group, click **New Window**.
2. Arrange the open windows. In each window, scroll to a part of the presentation that you want to display.

Reuse slides from other presentations

There are multiple ways to reuse slides from one presentation in another:

- You can move or copy slides directly between open presentations.
- You can import slides from one presentation into another by using the Reuse Slides tool. It isn't necessary to open the source presentation.
- If you know in advance that you'll want to use a slide in multiple presentations, you can publish it to the slide library on your computer and then reuse it from there, without having to track down the presentation or undo any presentation-specific modifications that you might have made to the slide.

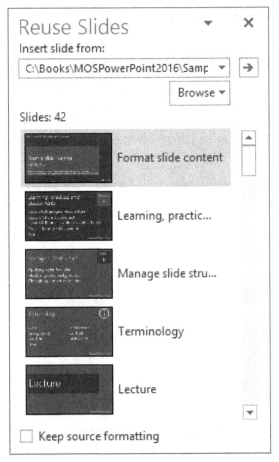

You can reuse slides from any presentation that you can browse to from File Explorer

To reuse slides from an existing presentation

1. In the **Thumbnails** pane or **Slide Sorter** pane, click where you want to insert the reused slide or slides.

2. On the **Home** tab or **Insert** tab, in the **Slides** group, click the **New Slide** arrow, and then click **Reuse Slides**.

3. In the **Reuse Slides** pane, click **Browse**, and then click **Browse File**.

4. In the **Browse** dialog box, locate and double-click the presentation containing the slides you want to reuse.

5. In the **Reuse Slides** pane, click each slide you want to reuse, and then close the pane.

Tip By default, reused slides take on the formatting of the presentation into which they are inserted. To retain the slides' source formatting, select the Keep Source Formatting check box before inserting the first slide.

Compare, combine, and review differences

Exam Strategy Viewing, accepting, and rejecting revisions in PowerPoint is not as intuitive as it is in Microsoft Word. Take some time to practice making changes to a presentation and comparing it with the original version to become familiar with ways of working with this feature.

You can compare two versions of the same presentation by merging changes made in one version into the other. The differences are recorded in the combined presentation as revisions. You can view the suggested changes and then accept or reject them.

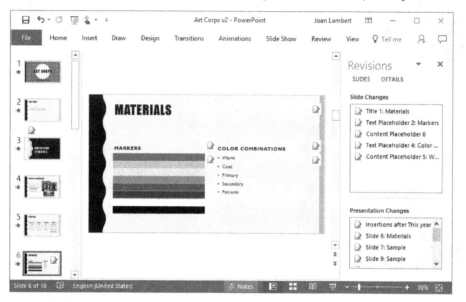

Icons in the Thumbnails, Slide, and Revision panes indicate content and structure changes

To combine two versions of the same presentation

1. With one version open, on the **Review** tab, in the **Compare** group, click **Compare**.

2. In the **Choose File to Merge with Current Presentation** dialog box, locate and double-click the version you want to combine.

To review revisions

→ On the slide, click any revision icon to display revision details.

Or

1. In the **Revisions** pane (which opens automatically after you combine two versions), display the **Details** page.
2. In the **Slide Changes** box, click any revision to display details.
3. On the **Review** tab, in the **Compare** group, click **Next** to move to the next slide with changes.

Or

1. In the **Revisions** pane, display the **Slides** page.
2. In the **Thumbnails** pane, click any slide to display the original version in the Slide pane and the modified version in the Revisions pane.

To accept or reject revisions

→ With a revision active, on the **Review** tab, in the **Compare** group, click **Accept** or **Reject**.

→ On the **Slides** page of the **Revisions** pane, point to a revised slide, and then click **Accept Changes** or **Reject Changes**.

→ In the ScreenTip displaying the revision details for an object, do any of the following:

- Select the **All changes to** check box to implement all changes to the object.
- Select the check box of an individual revision to implement the change.
- Clear the check box of a revision to reject the change.

To complete the review process

→ On the **Review** tab, in the **Compare** group, click **End Review** to discard unaccepted changes and all markup.

Tip To accept changes without displaying the details, on the Review tab, in the Compare group, click the Accept arrow, and then click Accept All Changes To This Slide or Accept All Changes To The Presentation. If you change your mind, in the Compare group, click the Reject arrow, and then click Reject All Changes To This Slide or Reject All Changes To The Presentation.

Manage comments

If you are asked to review a presentation, you can give feedback about a slide, without disrupting its text and layout, by inserting a comment. If you add a comment without first selecting an object on the slide, a small comment icon appears in the upper-left corner of the slide. If you select an object before adding the comment, the comment icon appears in the upper-right corner of the object.

You add comments in the Comments pane, where comments are identified by the user name specified on the General page of the PowerPoint Options dialog box. You can work with the Comments pane open, or close it until you need it again.

5

Closing the Comments pane leaves the comment icons on the slide. Clicking a comment icon opens the Comments pane and displays the selected comment.

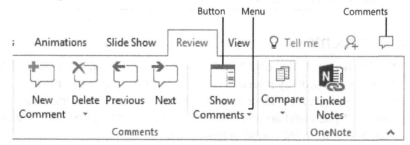

A comment icon appears next to the active slide element

You can turn the display of comments on and off and move quickly back and forth among the comments by using the commands in the Comments group on the Review tab. You can reply to comments to create a focused conversation about a slide or slide object. You can delete comments individually, delete all the comments on a slide, or delete all the comments in a presentation.

To open the Comments pane

➜ On the **Review** tab, in the **Comments** group, click the **Show Comments** button (not the arrow, which opens a menu of options).

➜ To the right of the ribbon tabs, click the **Comments** button.

Quickly access the Comments pane by clicking the Comments button

---

Tip The Comments button was added to the ribbon in an update to PowerPoint 2016. If you don't subscribe to Office updates, your installation of PowerPoint might not include this button.

To insert a comment

1. Click the slide or object on the slide to which you want to attach a comment.
2. On the **Review** tab, in the **Comments** group, click **New Comment**.
3. In the **Comments** pane, enter the comment in the box that opens.

To display the subject of a specific comment

→ In the **Comments** pane, click the comment icon.

To close the Comments pane

→ Click the **Close** button in the upper-right corner of the **Comments** pane to close the pane.

To display and hide comment icons on slides

→ On the **Review** tab, in the **Comments** group, click the **Show Comments** arrow, and then on the **Show Comments** menu, click **Show Markup**.

To move among comments

→ In the **Comments** pane, click **Previous** or **Next**.

→ On the **Review** tab, in the **Comments** group, click **Previous** or **Next**.

To edit a comment

→ In the **Comments** pane, click the comment, and then modify the text.

To reply to a comment

→ In the **Comments** pane, click the **Reply** box for the comment, and then enter your reply.

To delete a specific comment

→ Right-click the comment icon, and then click **Delete Comment**.

→ Click the comment icon, and then on the **Review** tab, in the **Comments** group, click **Delete**.

→ In the **Comments** pane, point to the comment, and then click the **Delete** button (the **X**) that appears.

To delete all the comments on the current slide

→ On the **Review** tab, in the **Comments** group, click the **Delete** arrow, and then click **Delete All Comments and Ink on This Slide**.

To delete all the comments in the presentation

1. On the **Review** tab, in the **Comments** group, click the **Delete** arrow, and then click **Delete All Comments and Ink in This Presentation**.
2. To confirm the deletion, click **Yes**.

5

Objective 5.1 practice tasks

The practice files for these tasks are located in the **MOSPowerPoint2016
\Objective5** practice file folder. The folder also contains result files that
you can use to check your work.

➤ Open the **PowerPoint_5-1a** and **PowerPoint_5-1b** presentations, and
do the following:

- ❑ Arrange the open presentations side by side.

- ❑ After slide 4 of the **PowerPoint_5-1a** presentation, insert slide 5
  from the **PowerPoint_5-1b** presentation by dragging it into the
  presentation.

- ❑ Close the **PowerPoint_5-1b** presentation.

- ❑ At the end of the **PowerPoint_5-1a** presentation, insert the slide title
  Goals for the Coming Year from the **PowerPoint_5-1b** presentation
  by using the Reuse Slides command.

- ❑ Open a second instance of the presentation in a separate program
  window, and arrange the two instances side by side.

- ❑ Display slide 4 in the left instance, and slide 5 in the right instance.
  Verify that the merged slide has taken on the formatting of the
  presentation.

➤ Save the **PowerPoint_5-1a** presentation. Open the **PowerPoint_5-1a_
results** presentation. Compare the two presentations to check your
work. Then close the open presentations.

➤ Open the **PowerPoint_5-1c** presentation, and do the following:

- ❑ Compare and combine the presentation with the **PowerPoint_5-1d**
  presentation from the practice file folder.

- ❑ Review the marked differences; click Next to move between
  changes, and select each set of changes to display them on the slide.

- ❑ Reject the changes on slides 2 and 7. Accept the presentation
  changes (the theme and additional content). Then end the review.

➤ Save the **PowerPoint_5-1c** presentation.

➤ Open the **PowerPoint_5-1c_results** presentation. Compare the two
presentations to check your work. Then close the open presentations.

➤ Open the **PowerPoint_5-1e** presentation and do the following:

- ❏ Delete the comment attached to the title slide.
- ❏ Review the remaining comments in the presentation.
- ❏ Using only one command, delete all the remaining comments.
- ❏ In the header of slide 2, insert the comment <u>Change date to reflect that of workshop</u>.
- ❏ On slide 9, attach the comment <u>Is newer data available?</u> to the citation.
- ❏ On slide 13, attach the comment <u>Native plant graphics would add interest</u> to the content placeholder, and then click away from the comment to close it.
- ❏ On slide 13, edit the comment to read <u>Colorful native plant graphics would make this more interesting</u>.

➤ Save the **PowerPoint_5-1e** presentation. Open the **PowerPoint_5-1e_ results** presentation. Compare the two presentations to check your work. Then close the open presentations.

Objective 5.2: Finalize presentations

Protect presentations

After you finish preparing a presentation for distribution, you can mark it as final. This feature saves the file, deactivates most PowerPoint tools, and displays an information bar at the top of the screen to indicate that no further changes should be made to the presentation. However, you can easily override the final status and make changes to the presentation.

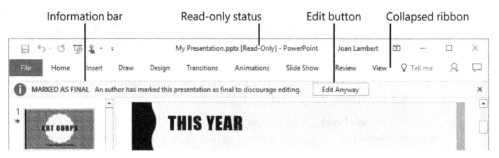

PowerPoint hides the ribbon after marking a presentation as final

The simplest way to control access to a presentation is to assign a password to it. You can assign two types of passwords:

- **Password to open** Assigning this type of password encrypts the presentation so that only people with the password can open and view it.

Simple encryption protects the file

To open a presentation that requires a password to open, you must enter the exact password, including capitalization, numbers, spaces, and symbols.

- **Password to modify** Assigning this type of password does not encrypt the presentation. Users can open the presentation in read-only mode or enter a password to open the presentation in edit mode.

Prevent users from modifying the file

To open a presentation that requires a password only to modify, you can either enter the exact password to open and modify it or open a version that you can view but not modify.

To mark a presentation as final

1. On the **Info** page of the Backstage view, click **Protect Presentation**, and then click **Mark as Final**.

2. In the message box, click **OK**, and then click **OK** in the confirmation box.

To turn off the final status

→ In the information bar below the ribbon, click **Edit Anyway**.

→ On the **Info** page of the Backstage view, click **Protect Presentation**, and then click **Mark as Final**.

To set a password for a presentation

1. On the **Info** page of the Backstage view, click **Protect Presentation**, and then click **Encrypt with Password**.

2. In the **Encrypt Document** and **Confirm Password** dialog boxes, enter the password you want to assign, and then click **OK**.

Or

1. In the **Save As** dialog box, click **Tools**, and then click **General Options**.

2. In the **General Options** dialog box, in the **Password to open** or **Password to modify** box, enter the password you want, and then click **OK**.

3. In the **Confirm Password** dialog box, reenter the password you previously entered, and then click **OK**.

4. In the **Save As** dialog box, click **Save**.

To change the password of an open presentation

1. On the **Info** page of the Backstage view, click **Protect Presentation**, and then click **Encrypt with Password**.

2. In the **Encrypt Document** dialog box, change the password, and then click **OK**.

3. In the **Confirm Password** dialog box, reenter the password you entered in the previous step, and then click **OK**.

Or

1. In the **General Options** dialog box, change the entry in the **Password to open** or **Password to modify** box, and then click **OK**.

2. In the **Confirm Password** dialog box, reenter the new password, and then click **OK**.

3. In the **Save As** dialog box, click **Save**.

To delete the password of an open presentation

1. On the **Info** page of the Backstage view, click **Protect Presentation**, and then click **Encrypt with Password**.

2. In the **Encrypt Document** dialog box, delete the password, and then click **OK**.

Or

1. In the **General Options** dialog box, delete either or both passwords, and then click **OK**.

2. In the **Save As** dialog box, click **Save**.

Inspect presentations for issues

PowerPoint includes three tools that you can use to inspect a presentation for possible problems before you distribute it electronically (as a file): The Document Inspector, the Accessibility Checker, and the Compatibility Checker.

The Document Inspector checks for content and information that you might not want to share with readers, such as:

- Information that identifies the presentation authors
- Tracked changes, comments, and ink annotations
- Other files (such as documents) that are embedded within the presentation you're inspecting
- Content add-ins and Task Pane add-ins that might not be available to presentation viewers
- Macros, form controls, and ActiveX controls saved as part of the file
- Built-in and custom file properties
- File version history and server properties

The Document Inspector offers to remove content that it locates, but doesn't provide specifics. You can opt to remove or retain any category of content. There are some types of content that you might want to keep and review individually.

The Document Inspector provides pass/fail results for each category you choose

The Accessibility Checker identifies slide elements and formatting that might be difficult for people with certain kinds of disabilities to read or for assistive devices such as screen readers to access. These issues are divided by decreasing severity into three classifications: Errors, Warnings, and Tips. In PowerPoint presentations, the Accessibility Checker inspects content to ensure that it meets the criteria shown in the following table.

Error rules	Warning rules	Tip rules
All non-text content has alternative text Tables specify column header information All slides have titles	Hyperlink text is meaningful Table has a simple structure Tables don't use blank cells for formatting	Closed captions are included for inserted audio and video The reading order of a slide should be logical Slide titles in a deck are unique

See Also For detailed information about these and other Accessibility Checker rules, go to *https://support.office.microsoft.com/en-us/article/Rules-used-by-the-Accessibility-Checker-651e08f2-0fc3-4e10-aaca-74b4a67101c1* (or go to *https://support.office.microsoft.com* and search for "Accessibility Checker rules"). For more information about designing documents for accessibility, display the Accessibility Checker pane, and then at the bottom of the pane, click the Read More link.

From the Accessibility Checker pane, you can select any issue to display information about why it might be a problem and how to fix it. You can leave the Accessibility Checker open while you work—its contents will automatically update to indicate the current issues.

Accessibility Checker   ▾   ✕

Inspection Results

Errors

▷ Missing Alt Text (1)

▷ No Header Row Specified (1)

Warnings

▷ Blank Table Rows or Columns (1)

Tips

▷ Duplicate Slide Title (4)

◢ Check Reading Order

Slide 4

Additional Information   ⌄

Why Fix: ▲

People who cannot view the slide will hear slide text, shapes, and content read back in a specific order. You should verify that the reading order and labels will make sense in the order they will be read back.

How To Fix:

To check the order content will be read back: 1) Switch to the Home tab, click Arrange, and   ▾

Select and fix each issue listed above to make this document accessible for people with disabilities.

Read more about making documents accessible

The Accessibility Checker pane provides links directly to possible issues

Tip After you run the Accessibility Checker, information about presentation content issues is also shown in the Inspect Presentation area of the Info page of the Backstage view.

The Compatibility Checker identifies formatting and features that aren't supported or won't work as expected in PowerPoint 2010 and earlier versions. Fixing these issues ensures that the appearance and functionality of the document will be consistent for all readers.

Microsoft PowerPoint Compatibility Checker	? ✕

ⓘ The following features in this presentation are not supported by earlier versions of PowerPoint. These features may be lost or degraded when you save this presentation in an earlier file format.

Summary	Occurrences
The SmartArt graphic and any text in it cannot be edited when using versions of Microsoft Office earlier than Office 2007. (Slide 5)	1 _Help_
Slide master and layout level guides will be lost.	2 _Help_
Reply comments will be converted to top-level comments and will no longer be grouped by comment thread.	1 _Help_

☑ Check compatibility when saving in PowerPoint 97-2003 formats.

OK

The Compatibility Checker pane provides information about possible issues

The following PowerPoint 2016 presentation content features aren't supported by some earlier versions of PowerPoint:

- SmartArt graphics
- Tables that contain WordArt or have specific formatting applied
- Unsupported formatting effects (Reflection, Glow, Bevel, Soft Edges, 3-D Rotation, or Fills) applied to shapes or shape text
- Unsupported WordArt effects applied to text
- ActiveX controls, customized prompt text, and placeholder animation on custom slide layouts
- Uninitialized ActiveX controls

If you share presentations with people who are using a version of PowerPoint earlier than 2007, they can install the free Microsoft Office Compatibility Pack for Word, Excel, and PowerPoint File Formats from the Microsoft Download Center at *https://download.microsoft.com*. The Compatibility Pack doesn't provide additional functionality in the older program version, but it does enable users to open .pptx files in the older version of PowerPoint.

5

To inspect a presentation for common issues

1. Save the presentation, and then display the **Info** page of the Backstage view.

2. In the **Inspect Presentation** area of the **Info** page, click **Check for Issues**, and then click **Inspect Document** to open the Document Inspector dialog box, which lists the items that will be checked.

3. Clear the check boxes for any groups of properties you don't want to check for, and then click **Inspect** to display a report on the presence of the properties you selected.

   In addition to the basic properties that are displayed in the Properties section of the Info page, the inspector might return information about comments, annotations, hidden and off-slide content, and speaker notes.

4. Review the results, and then click the **Remove All** button for any category of information that you want to remove.

   > **Tip** You can choose to retain content identified by the Document Inspector if you know that it is appropriate for distribution.

5. In the **Document Inspector** dialog box, click **Reinspect**, and then click **Inspect** to verify the removal of the properties and other data you selected.

6. When you're satisfied with the results, close the **Document Inspector** dialog box.

To inspect a presentation for accessibility issues

1. On the **Info** page of the Backstage view, click **Check For Issues**, and then click **Check Accessibility** to run the Accessibility Checker.

2. In the **Accessibility Checker** pane, review the inspection results and make any changes you want to the document.

3. When you finish, do either of the following:

   - Click the **X** in the upper-right corner of the **Accessibility Checker** pane to close the pane.

   - Leave the pane open to continue checking for accessibility issues as you work with the document.

To inspect a presentation for compatibility issues

1. Save the presentation.

2. On the **Info** page of the Backstage view, click **Check for Issues**, and then click **Check Compatibility**. The window immediately displays a list of content issues that aren't compatible with earlier versions of PowerPoint.

To correct compatibility issues

1. Review the issue description and note the number of instances of the issue within the document. Some issues include a Help link to additional information.

2. Locate the named element by searching or scanning the presentation slides, and then remove or modify it to meet the compatibility requirements.

3. When you finish, click **OK** to close the Compatibility Checker.

To maintain backward compatibility with a previous version of PowerPoint

1. When saving the presentation, choose the previous file format in the **Save as type** list.

2. In the **Microsoft PowerPoint Compatibility Checker** window, click **Continue** to convert the unsupported features.

Proof presentations

The AutoCorrect feature detects and automatically corrects many common capitalization and spelling errors, such as *teh* instead of *the* or *WHen* instead of *When*. You can customize AutoCorrect to recognize words you frequently misspell.

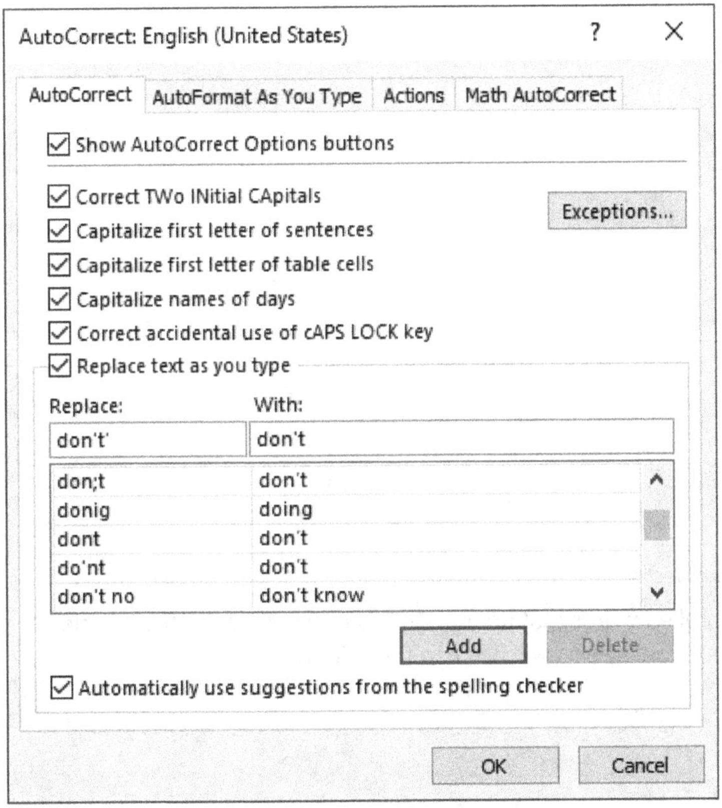

You can add your own frequent misspellings to the AutoCorrect list

---

Tip You can also use AutoCorrect entries to automate the typing of frequently used text, such as replacing an abbreviation of a company name with the full name of the company.

By default, PowerPoint checks the spelling of anything you enter against its built-in dictionary. To draw attention to a word that is not in its dictionary and that might be misspelled, PowerPoint underlines it with a red wavy underline.

Tip To turn off the display of red wavy lines, clear the Check Spelling As You Type check box on the Proofing page of the PowerPoint Options dialog box.

You can correct the marked spelling errors immediately or ignore the red wavy under-lines and instead handle all the potential misspellings in the presentation at one time by clicking options in the Spelling pane.

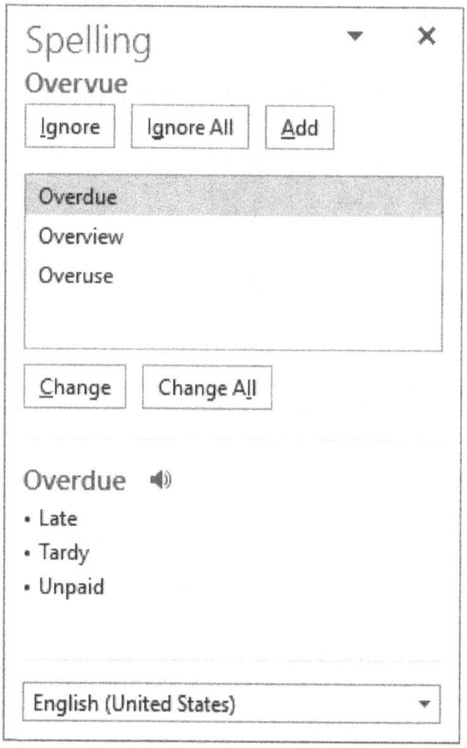

The spelling checker suggests corrections

You can add correctly spelled words that are flagged as misspellings to the supple-mental dictionary so that PowerPoint will not flag them in the future.

To add an entry and its replacement to the AutoCorrect list

1. On the **Proofing** page of the **PowerPoint Options** dialog box, in the **AutoCorrect options** area, click **AutoCorrect Options**.
2. On the **AutoCorrect** tab of the **AutoCorrect** dialog box, enter the misspelling in the **Replace** box.
3. Enter the correction in the **With** box.
4. Click **Add**, and then click **OK**.

To correct a word that is marked by a red wavy underline

➜ Right-click the word, and then click the suggested replacement you want.

To check the spelling of the entire presentation at one time

1. On the **Review** tab, in the **Proofing** group, click **Spelling**.
2. For each word PowerPoint flags, do one of the following in the **Spelling** pane:
   - To ignore the flagged word, click **Ignore** or **Ignore All**.
   - To change the flagged word, click a suggested correction, or enter the correction in the **Change to** box. Then click either **Change** or **Change All**.
   - To delete a duplicated word, click **Delete**.
   - To add a word to the supplemental dictionary, click **Add**.

Preserve presentation content

Before you share a media-intensive presentation with other people, you might want to compress the media to make the presentation file smaller and more portable. PowerPoint offers three levels of compression.

Compress Media			? ✕
Slide	Name	Initial Size (MB)	Status
1	BackgroundMusic	9	Complete - 5.2 MB Saved
7	Joan Lambert - Wednesday, April 6, 2016 ...	3.2	Already Compressed
8	SoundEffect	7.9	Complete - 3.6 MB Saved
9	001-1	26	Complete - 0.2 MB Saved
11	001-2	15.8	Complete - 0.2 MB Saved
13	001-3	7.5	Complete - 0.2 MB Saved

Compression complete. You saved 9.4 MB.

Close

If an audio or video clip has already been compressed, the Compress Media tool doesn't change it

5

If your presentation uses specialized fonts that might not be available on a viewer's computer, you can embed the fonts in the presentation to ensure that the presentation content appears as you intend it to.

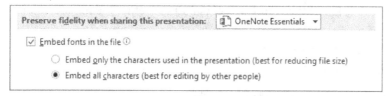

Embedding fonts is particularly important when a presentation uses corporate licensed fonts

To compress media

→ On the **Info** page of the Backstage view, click **Compress Media**, and then click **Presentation Quality**, **Internet Quality**, or **Low Quality**.

> **IMPORTANT** The Compress Media button appears on the Info page only if the presentation contains audio clips or video clips.

To reverse a compression operation

→ On the **Info** page of the Backstage view, click **Compress Media**, and then click **Undo**.

To embed fonts in a presentation

1. On the **Save** page of the **PowerPoint Options** dialog box, in the **Preserve fidelity when sharing this presentation** section, select the **Embed fonts in the file** check box.

2. Do either of the following, and then click **OK**:
   - To embed only the characters that are necessary for the current version of the presentation, click **Embed only the characters used in the presentation**.
   - To embed all characters of all fonts that are present in the presentation so that they are available to another person who works with the presentation, click **Embed all characters**.

3. Save the modified presentation, or save a copy of the presentation that is for the express purpose of distribution, and close the smaller original file without saving the changes.

Export presentations to other formats

If you intend to run your presentation on a computer other than the one on which you developed it, you need to ensure that the fonts, linked objects, and any other necessary items are available to the presentation. You can use the Package For CD feature to save all presentation components to a CD (not a DVD) or other type of removable media. You can include more than one presentation, and you can specify the order in which the presentations should run. As part of the packaging process, you can assign a password and remove extraneous information from the packaged file.

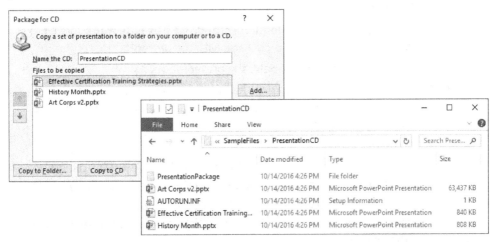

You can package the files required by multiple presentations

After PowerPoint assembles the files, it creates a folder of supporting files and adds an autorun file. When you insert the presentation CD into your CD/DVD drive, the AutoPlay dialog box opens so that you can run the presentation.

If you want to deliver your presentation to a wider audience, you can use one of the following methods:

- Save the presentation as a video that is optimized for web delivery, and post the video online.

- Deliver the presentation online through the Office Presentation Service. You can use this free service to share a presentation live and make it available for download during or after the presentation.

Tip The Office Presentation Service is free; you must have a Microsoft account to connect to it, but if you're already logged on to your computer with your Microsoft account, the service picks up that information automatically.

To package a presentation for delivery on another computer

1. On the **Export** page of the Backstage view, click **Package Presentation for CD**, and then click **Package for CD**.

2. In the **Package for CD** dialog box, provide a disc name in the **Name the CD** box, and then click **Options**.

> **Tip** The disc name is shown as the drive name in File Explorer when the disc is in the disc drive.

3. In the **Options** dialog box, do any of the following, and then click **OK**:

   - Select or clear the **Linked files** and **Embedded TrueType fonts** check boxes to specify which elements to package with the presentation.

   - Set passwords to open or modify the presentation.

   - If you want to run the Document Inspector before packaging the presentation, select the **Inspect presentations for inappropriate or private information** check box.

4. Do either of the following:

   - Insert a blank CD in your CD/DVD burner, and if the **AutoPlay** dialog box opens, close it. Then in the **Package for CD** dialog box, click **Copy to CD**.

   - In the **Package for CD** dialog box, click **Copy to Folder**. In the **Copy to Folder** dialog box, specify the folder in which you want to store the package, and then click **OK**.

5. If you selected the **Linked files** check box in step 3, click **Yes** in the Microsoft PowerPoint dialog box to verify that you trust the source of the linked content.

6. If you selected the **Inspect presentations...** check box in step 3, follow the steps in the Document Inspector, and then click **Close**.

7. When a message box indicates that the packaging operation was successful, click **No** to indicate that you don't want to copy the same package again, and then click **Close**.

To package a presentation as a video

1. On the **Export** page of the Backstage view, click **Create a Video**.

2. On the **Create a Video** page, click **Presentation Quality**, **Internet Quality**, or **Low Quality** in the first list.

3. If you have recorded timings or narration with the presentation, select either **Use Recorded Timings and Narrations** or **Don't Use Recorded Timings and Narrations** in the second list, to indicate whether to package those elements with the video.

Tip If you want to record the timings and narration now, you can start that process from the second list or from the Slide Show tab.

---

4. If you selected the **Don't Use...** option in step 3, in the **Seconds spent on each slide** box, enter the time to display each slide.

5. On the **Create a Video** page, click **Create Video**.

6. In the **Save As** dialog box, do the following, and then click **Save**:

   a. Browse to the folder in which you want to save the video.

   b. Enter a name for the video in the **File name** box.

   c. Click **MPEG-4 Video** or **Windows Media Video** in the **Save as type** list.

To share a presentation through the Office Presentation Service

1. On the **Share** page of the Backstage view, click **Present Online**.

2. In the **Present Online** pane, if a list at the top contains multiple online presentation options, click **Office Presentation Service** in the list.

3. If you want to make the presentation available for download, select the **Enable remote viewers to download the presentation** check box.

4. Click **Present Online**.

5. Read the terms, and then click **Connect**.

6. After the service connects by using your Microsoft account, click **Copy Link** or **Send in Email**, and provide the presentation link to your intended viewers. Then click **Start Presentation**.

5

Objective 5.2 practice tasks

The practice file for these tasks is located in the **MOSPowerPoint2016 \Objective5** practice file folder. The folder also contains a result file that you can use to check your work.

➤ Open the **PowerPoint_5-2** presentation and do the following:

- ❏ On slide 2, correct the spelling of *infermation*.
- ❏ Check the spelling of the entire presentation, correcting any mistakes that the spelling checker identifies.
- ❏ Add the term *CSCom* to the dictionary.
- ❏ Add the correct spelling of *employes* to the AutoCorrect substitution table.
- ❏ Use the Document Inspector to locate and remove all identifying and tracking information and comments from the file. Leave the speaker notes in the presentation.
- ❏ Assign the password P@ssword to the presentation so that the file can be opened but not changed.
- ❏ Save the presentation with the name MyPassword, and close it.

➤ Open a read-only version of the password-protected *MyPassword* presentation and do the following:

- ❏ Verify that it's not possible to edit the content.
- ❏ Close the file, and then open a version you can edit.
- ❏ Remove the password from the file, and save it as PowerPoint_5-2a.pptx.

➤ In the **PowerPoint_5-2a** presentation, do the following:

- ❏ Using the Package for CD tool, export the presentation to a package named MyPackage and save it in the practice file folder.
- ❏ Mark the presentation as final.

➤ Save the presentation as PowerPoint_5-2b.pptx.

➤ Open the **PowerPoint_5-2_results** presentation. Compare the two presentations to check your work. Then close the open presentations.

Index

About the author

JOAN LAMBERT has worked closely with Microsoft technologies since 1986, and in the training and certification industry since 1997. As President and CEO of Online Training Solutions, Inc. (OTSI), Joan guides the translation of technical information and requirements into useful, relevant, and measurable resources for people who are seeking certification of their computer skills or who simply want to know how to get things done efficiently.

Joan is the author or coauthor of more than four dozen books about Windows and Office (for Windows, Mac, and iPad), five generations of Microsoft Office Specialist certification study guides, video-based training courses for SharePoint and OneNote, QuickStudy guides for Windows and Office, and the GO! series book for Outlook 2016.

Blissfully based in America's Finest City, Joan is a Microsoft Certified Professional, Microsoft Office Specialist Master (for all versions of Office since Office 2003), Microsoft Certified Technology Specialist (for Windows and Windows Server), Microsoft Certified Technology Associate (for Windows), Microsoft Dynamics Specialist, and Microsoft Certified Trainer.

ONLINE TRAINING SOLUTIONS, INC. (OTSI) specializes in the design and creation of Microsoft Office, SharePoint, and Windows training solutions and the production of online and printed training resources. For more information about OTSI, visit *www.otsi.com* or for advance information about upcoming training resources and informative tidbits about technology and publishing, follow us on Facebook at *www.facebook.com/Online.Training.Solutions.Inc.*

Acknowledgments

I am extremely grateful for the unflagging support and contributions of Jaime Odell, Kathy Krause, and Susie Carr at OTSI—this book (and so many others) wouldn't exist without our fabulous team! Thank you also to Rosemary Caperton and Kim Spilker at Microsoft Press, and Laura Norman at Pearson Education, for making the MOS Study Guide series for Office 2016 a reality.

Finally, I am so very grateful for the support of my daughter, Trinity. Her confidence, encouragement, and terrific cooking when I'm working late bring me great joy.

Now that you've read the book...

Tell us what you think!

Was it useful?
Did it teach you what you wanted to learn?
Was there room for improvement?

Let us know at https://aka.ms/tellpress

Your feedback goes directly to the staff at Microsoft Press,
and we read every one of your responses. Thanks in advance!